Get the GRADE!
AQA GCSE English
LITERATURE

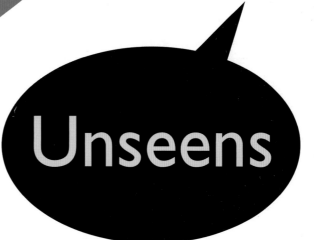

WORKING
with the **Poetry**
Anthology

AND THE

Unseens

Alan Howe

Series Editors:
Sue Bennett
Dave Stockwin

DYNAMIC
LEARNING

HODDER
EDUCATION
AN HACHETTE UK COMPANY

Photo credits and acknowledgements can be found on page 139.

Although every effort has been made to ensure that website addresses are correct at time of going to press, Hodder Education cannot be held responsible for the content of any website mentioned. It is sometimes possible to find a relocated web page by typing in the address of the home page for a website in the URL window of your browser.

Orders: please contact Bookpoint Ltd, 130 Milton Park, Abingdon, Oxon OX14 4SB. Telephone: (44) 01235 827720. Fax: (44) 01235 400454. Lines are open 9.00–17.00, Monday to Saturday, with a 24-hour message answering service. Visit our website at www.hoddereducation.co.uk

© Alan Howe 2015

First published in 2015 by

Hodder Education

An Hachette UK Company,

338 Euston Road

London NW1 3BH

Impression number	5	4	3	2	1
Year		2019	2018	2017	2016	2015

Typeset in PMN Caecilia Light 9.5pt by DC Graphic Design Ltd., Swanley Village, UK

Printed in Italy

A catalogue record for this title is available from the British Library

ISBN 9781471832888

CONTENTS

THE ANTHOLOGY

THE UNSEENS

Introduction

⇨ GCSE English Literature for AQA

The reformed specification for English Literature is designed to encourage the reading of 'a wide range of classic literature', both contemporary works and those from the literary heritage. Students will be tested on their responses to a Shakespeare play, a nineteenth-century novel, modern prose or drama, and the comparison of 15 studied poems as well as the comparison of two unseen poems. In this book we hope to assist students and teachers to meet the challenges of the poetry section of the examination and offer candidates the opportunity to achieve at the highest possible level.

⇨ Assessment objectives

There are four assessment objectives, common to all examination boards, which are as follows:

AO1	Read, understand and respond to texts. Students should be able to: • Maintain a critical style and develop an informed personal response • Use textual references, including quotations, to support and illustrate interpretations.	35–40%
AO2	Analyse the language, form and structure used by a writer to create meanings and effects, using relevant subject terminology where appropriate.	40–45%
AO3	Show understanding of the relationship between texts and the contexts in which they were written.	15–20%
AO4	Use a range of vocabulary and sentence structures for clarity, purpose and effect, with accurate spelling and punctuation.	5%

In each specification as a whole, 20–25% of the marks should require candidates to show the abilities described in AO1, AO2 and AO3 through tasks which require them to make **comparisons across texts**. In the case of AQA GCSE English Literature, this requirement to compare will be assessed on the **Poetry Section** of Paper 2. You should note that AO4 (Spelling, Punctuation and Grammar) is **not** assessed on either of the Poetry sections of Paper 2.

⇨ About the exam

Paper 2 will involve the comparison of poems from the AQA Anthology, a comparison of two unseen poems, and a response to fiction or drama from the British Isles from 1914 onwards. The paper will be **2 hours and 15 minutes** in length which means you should spend approximately **45 minutes** on each of the 3 sections.

The poetry sections are **Section B** and **Section C**.

Section B – The Anthology

The question that you must attempt in this section is based on your study of the AQA Poetry Anthology 'Poems past and present' which consists of **two** clusters of **15 poems** written between 1789 and the present day.

The 15 poems in each cluster are linked by theme. Cluster 1's theme is '**Love and Relationships**' and Cluster 2's theme is '**Power and Conflict**'. There will be one question on each cluster. Remember: you only need to answer **one** question on **one** of the two clusters.

This question is worth a total of **30 marks**.

What you have to do

No matter which of the two clusters you have studied, the question lay-out is the same. A list of all the poems in the cluster will be printed for you as a useful reminder of your possible choices. The question will ask you to compare a named poem, which will be printed for you, with another poem of your choice from the same cluster.

Obviously, this means that you must have a really good working knowledge of all the poems in your chosen cluster. Don't worry – this book will help you to gain just that!

Here are two examples of typical questions from Section B:

- Compare the ways poets present ideas about conflict in 'Bayonet Charge' and in **one** other poem from 'Power and Conflict'.
- Compare the ways poets present attitudes to love in 'The Farmer's Bride' and in **one** other poem from 'Love and Relationships'.

As you can see, the ability to compare is a key element of these questions but don't worry – this book will show you how to write a great comparison essay!

Section C – The Unseens

This section of the examination tests your ability to read, understand and compare two poems which you probably will not have seen before. The two poems will be linked by theme: for example, they might both be about school, family, animals, growing up, etc.

This question is worth a total of **32 marks**.

What you have to do

The Unseen section has a slightly different question format from Section B.

There are **two** questions to answer and you must answer them **both**.

Question 1 refers to the first of the two printed poems and requires you to write about the feelings and/or attitudes and/or ideas in the poem and how they are presented by the poet. This question is worth **24 marks**.

Question 2 refers to both of the printed poems and requires you to write about the similarities and differences between the ways the poets present their ideas/feelings/attitudes in the two poems. This question is worth **8 marks**.

All this might sound a little daunting but don't worry – this book will show you how to write a great unseen response!

Mark schemes

There are three mark schemes for the two poetry sections.

- The mark scheme for Section B (The Anthology) is divided into six levels, as is the mark scheme for Section C (The Unseen) Question 1.
- The mark scheme for Section C (The Unseen) Question 2 is divided into four levels.

A 'student-friendly' version of the mark scheme is available on Dynamic Learning. AQA mark schemes are worth reading to give you an idea of the sort of things your examiner will be looking for. These are available on the AQA website.

Cluster 1: Love and Relationships

*In secret we met –
In silence I grieve*

'When We Two Parted' by Lord Byron

The poem was first published in 1816. The poet writes about a love affair that has ended.

⇨ First impressions

The poem directly addresses the 'other' person in the relationship.

① Read Verse 1. Choose four or five words from the poem that provide clues about the poet's state of mind.

② Now read the rest of the poem.

- Verse 2: what does the poet feel 'now'?
- Verse 3: what might the poet not be able to 'tell'?
- Verse 4: what does the poet seem to be most upset about?

Lord Byron

KEY VOCAB

foretold – told about before it takes place, prophesied

knell – sound of a bell, especially a bell rung at a funeral

rue – repent, wish something had never happened, feel dejected and sad

⇨ Look a little closer

① 'When We Two Parted' is a poem that doesn't directly reveal all of its secrets. As you read through the poem, note down **questions** that the poem raises. For example, here is how one student annotated Verse 1:

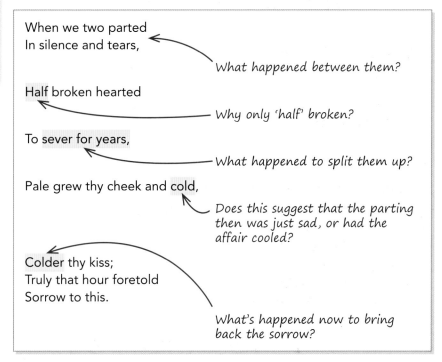

When we two parted
In silence and tears,

What happened between them?

Half broken hearted

Why only 'half' broken?

To sever for years,

What happened to split them up?

Pale grew thy cheek and cold,

Does this suggest that the parting then was just sad, or had the affair cooled?

Colder thy kiss;
Truly that hour foretold
Sorrow to this.

What's happened now to bring back the sorrow?

② When you have completed your list of questions, look back through the poem and speculate about the kind of events that might have occurred to give rise to the feelings that the poet expresses.

Consider the following questions:

a) What might have happened to make the poet remember and re-live his emotions and recollections of the first parting?

b) Who might 'They' be – mentioned twice in Verse 3?

c) Why might the poet decide to continue to 'grieve' in silence?

d) What seems to upset the writer most about what has happened?

⇨ Exploring the detail

The poem explores the poet's feelings about an affair that has turned out badly. Part of the poem's success is in the way that the writer conveys his feelings using a strict poetic structure, tightly controlled rhyme and metre, and repetition of certain key words and phrases. Use the following questions and prompts to identify, and develop your understanding of how these features add to the poem's effect on the reader.

1 Read the poem aloud several times.

- As you read, think about where the stresses fall on the words. For example, in the opening lines of Verse 1, you could read it by stressing the following words (shown in bold):

> **When** we two **parted**
> In **silence** and **tears,**
> **Half** broken **hearted**
> To **sever** for **years,**

- Note that the stresses often fall on words that build up a picture of the poet's feelings towards his long lost love. List these words or highlight them on a copy of the poem.

2 Find all the examples of words that convey cold or lack of life or colour. What do these suggest to you about the kind of feelings that the poet has?

3 The poem hinges on reflections about 'then' and 'now'. Find three examples from the poem where 'then' and 'now' are set in direct contrast to each other.

4 Consider the following examples of repetition. For each, explain its effect on the reader:

- *cold/colder* (Verse 1)
- *fame/name/shame/name* (Verses 2 and 3)
- *knew thee/knew thee too well* (Verse 3)
- *Long, long* (Verse 3, and a third repeat of 'long' in the final verse)
- *In secret we met – /In silence I grieve* (Verse 4)
- *Silence and tears* (Verses 1 and 4).

5 Now read the poem aloud again in two different ways:

- In a tone of sadness and sorrow that your love has grown cold towards you and is involved with another person.
- In a tone of increasing bitterness and anger about the ending of the affair and what the previous lover is now up to.

As you do this, think particularly about how you might read/say the following lines:

> *Thy vows are all broken*
> *And light is thy fame;*
>
> *A shudder comes o'er me –*
> *Why wert thou so dear?*
>
> *How should I greet thee? –*
> *With silence and tears.*

- Which 'reading' do you now consider to best convey the range of emotions that the poem expresses?

You should use your knowledge and understanding of the poem to provide a detailed written answer, and use quotations from the poem to provide evidence for your views.

1 The poem 'When We Two Parted' shows the poet's feelings linked to the break-up of a love affair. Show, by close reference to the poem, how you interpret the nature of the feelings expressed.

2 Write a detailed commentary on the poem, drawing out both what the poem reveals about the poet's feelings, what is hinted at about what happened, and explaining how the form and use of poetic devices create your understanding and interpretation.

3 Sad and sorrowful, or angry, self-centred ex-lover? Which of these descriptions best fit the persona of the writer of 'When We Two Parted'?

Key features

- Formal structure: four verses, each made up of two quatrains, with a regular rhyme scheme and careful use of metrical stresses to emphasise certain words and ideas
- Direct speaking voice, addressed to a second person who has no reply
- Contrasts between a time 'then' and the time 'now'
- Bleak, sorrowful or angry tone, with many references to parting, breaking and the death of a relationship

COMPARE WITH
- 'Neutral Tones'

Key themes

- Failure of a relationship
- Loss and parting

5 Why might the poet have used the phrase 'All things by **a law divine**' in Verse 1?

⇨ Exploring the detail

In what is quite a simple, short poem, Shelley uses some very effective techniques that add to its impact. Annotate a copy of the poem, using the following questions and prompts:

1 Highlight every reference to a feature of the natural world. For each, identify how Shelley uses personification to indicate how these aspects of nature behave or act.

2 The poem is full of repeated words or ideas. Annotate your copy to show:

- ideas of mixing or joining together in Verse 1
- kissing or physical intimacy in Verse 2.

What is the effect of these repeated words and phrases?

3 Investigate the way the poem uses differences in the rhythm of words and phrases – the metrical pattern of each line – to emphasise an idea.

Look for, highlight and comment on the effect of the:

- repetition of 'and '
- five monosyllables in the last line of Verse 1; 12 monosyllables in the final two lines of Verse 2

Percy Bysshe Shelley

❮ Nothing in the world is single ❯

'Love's Philosophy' by Percy Bysshe Shelley

The poem was first published in 1820, and was written by one of the most famous English poets of the Romantic period (late eighteenth and early nineteenth centuries). Romanticism favoured intuition over reason, individuals and the personal over the state, and saw meaning in and drew inspiration from the natural world. Poets and artists of this period believed in the creation of art by being responsive to feeling and emotion.

⇨ First impressions

'Philosophy' is the practice of seeking wisdom or knowledge about the nature of reality, attempting to understand why things are the way they are. Now, complete the following:

(1) Notice how Verse 1 starts with a series of five clear 'assertions' – statements written as if they were facts that can't be challenged or denied.

   a) On a copy of the poem, underline or highlight each assertion.
   b) Sum up the main point that the poet is making in Verse 1.

(2) Why do you think the poet ends each verse with a question?

⇨ Look a little closer

(1) Read the poem again.
(2) Look to the end of Verse 1. Who is the poet addressing?
(3) Make a list of all the language features that are similar in the two verses of the poem.
(4) Look at how the poet changes the order of 'I' and 'thine' in the last line of Verse 1 with 'thou' and 'me' in the final line of Verse 2. Explain how this use of words cleverly adds to the impact of the poem.

ℚ KEY VOCAB

fountains – used here to refer to a water spring that is the source of a stream or river

disdain – scorn or contempt; to look down, unfavourably, on another

9

- rhetorical questions
- repetition of 'sweet'. Which of these connotations of 'sweet' seems to best fit the way the word is used in the poem?

  attractive *charming* *sugary* *fresh*
  pleasurable *beautiful* *harmonious*

(4) Look closely at the use of punctuation at the end of lines. Read the poem aloud and experiment with the **pace** and **emphasis** that you give to each line, paying close attention to the punctuation marks. Look in particular at the use of the hyphen (–) towards the end of each verse. What does this suggest about how to read these final lines?

Tasks

1 How is the idea of 'love' presented in 'Love's Philosophy'?
2 Show how the poem uses logic, reason and a range of carefully controlled poetic devices to present this view.

Key features

- An argument presented in verse form
- Assertions about the natural world followed by a rhetorical question
- Use of personification and repetition to reinforce the main idea
- Changes to the rhythm of lines to drive the argument forwards

Key themes

- Human love and sexuality are part of the natural scheme of things
- Poetry can win another's affections

COMPARE WITH
- Sonnet 29 – 'I think of thee!'

Robert Browning

❝That moment she was mine, mine, fair,
Perfectly pure and good❞

'Porphyria's Lover' by Robert Browning

This poem was written in 1836. It is a dramatic monologue, in which a character, or 'persona', speaks to a silent listener. Browning was interested in exploring the minds of people who had an unusual or abnormal psychology in his dramatic monologues.

⇨ First impressions

(1) Think about the phrase 'dramatic monologue'. What do the two words suggest to you?

(2) Read the poem through as far as the line: 'Murmuring how she loved me –'

Make brief notes that record the:
- setting
- characters
- mood or atmosphere – and any changes you notice in this.

(3) Read on to the end of the poem.
- Identify the point at which the most significant action occurs.
- What does the speaker do following this?
- What does he think about what he has done? Find and highlight lines from the poem that indicate that he:

a) is pleased with his actions

b) thinks Porphyria is happy with his actions.

(4) Invent a **new title** for the poem that conveys your initial idea of its main theme.

11

⇨ Look a little closer

(1) On a copy of the poem, divide it into five sections as follows:

    a) From the beginning to 'heart fit to break'

    b) From 'When glided in Porphyria' to 'And called me.'

    c) From 'When no voice replied' to 'and all in vain:'

    d) From 'So, she was come through wind and rain.' to 'And strangled her.'

    e) From 'No pain felt she;' to the end of the poem

For each section, write a series of detailed **stage directions**, summing up where the scene takes place, the mood or atmosphere created, and describing the main action. For example, you might start with:

A man sits quite still, alone in a cold room in a cottage. Sound of rain and wind.

(2) To be a dramatic monologue:

- the poem must have a speaker and a silent listener
- the reader often recognises that there is a gap between what that speaker says and what he or she actually reveals.

Focus on what the poem reveals about the state of mind of the 'lover' – what he thinks, and what he believes.

Record your ideas and impressions as shown below:

The lover's actual words	What this reveals
I listened with heart fit to break	*He is desperately unhappy, or depressed by something*
Be sure I looked up at her eyes/Happy and proud	
That moment she was mine, mine,	
I am quite sure she felt no pain	
The smiling little rosy head,/So glad it has its utmost will	
And yet God has not said a word!	

(3) One student, commenting on the poem, wrote:

I have noticed that what happens when Porphyria arrives at the cottage is repeated, but in reverse, towards the end of the poem. I can't work out what this is meant to show.

- Look at the descriptions of what Porphyria does with her lover … and then at his actions after he's killed her.
- What is unusual about the way her actions are described?
- Explain what this student means by saying the actions happen 'in reverse, towards the end of the poem'.

KEY VOCAB

Porphyria – the woman in the poem is named after a disease called Porphyria. It is a rare type of disease where there is a problem with the production of haem (a substance that makes up haemoglobin in our blood) within the body which can result in abdominal pain, and problems with the nervous system and mental health

vex – to annoy or anger

dissever – to divide or break away

⇨ Exploring the detail

Look in detail at how the poem has been constructed.

(1) It has a regular rhyme scheme in five-line 'chunks'.

- Mark this on your copy of the poem for the first two five-line chunks.

(2) Each line is also written in a regular rhythm, using the iambic pentameter form.

- Read the first five lines aloud, and show how the stress falls in a regular pattern of five stresses.
- Why has the poet used the phrase 'early in' as opposed to the more usual construction 'in early'?

(3) Highlight all examples of the use of 'and'. Explain the effect of the repeated use of the conjunction 'and'. What might this reveal about the emotional state of mind of the murderer?

(4) What is the effect of the repeated references to 'yellow hair' in the opening 20 lines of the poem?

(5) Re-read the section that describes the actual murder, from: 'While I debated what to do' to 'And strangled her.'

- How would you describe the rhythm and tone of these lines?

(6) The form and structure of the poem creates a controlled, measured 'feel'.

- What does this suggest to you about the state of mind of the persona – the man who has just taken his lover's life by strangling her with her hair?

(7) The poem is an account, in the form of a murderer's confession. It is not so much a 'whodunit' as a 'why did he do it?' As the murderer tells his story, we can start to piece together what motivated him.

Search through the poem for clues as to what prompted him to kill Porphyria. Find and annotate with a brief note of explanation, lines that could reveal that he:

- is passive and doesn't respond to Porphyria's affections
- is upset that she hasn't been willing to give herself to him fully
- sees Porphyria as a person to be owned or possessed
- thinks Porphyria is seriously ill
- is doing the right thing in taking her life and feels no guilt
- believes she is happy that she has been murdered
- enjoys the outcome of his actions.

(8) Pull together all of the 'evidence' that you have gathered from the poem so far, and write a short paragraph in which you explain what, in your judgement, motivated the man to murder his loved one. In particular, explain why you think he decides to kill Porphyria at that **exact** moment.

Task

1   'Porphyria's Lover' is a poem that reveals the mind of a murderer. Write a detailed analysis of the poem, showing what we learn about the psychology of the killer, and commenting on how the poem's form, structure and use of language contribute to the creation of character.

Key features

- Dramatic monologue
- Regular form using a patterned rhyme scheme and iambic pentameters
- Reveals more about the main character than is actually said in the poem
- Description of weather and internal features in the cottage to create atmosphere and reveal a character's mood

Key themes

- How 'love' can be poisonous and destructive
- How women are portrayed in Victorian literature

COMPARE WITH

- 'The Farmer's Bride'

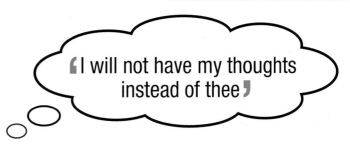

I will not have my thoughts instead of thee

Sonnet 29 – 'I think of thee!' by Elizabeth Barrett Browning

This is one of 44 sonnets in a collection entitled *Sonnets from the Portuguese*, which was published in 1850 but written some years earlier during Elizabeth Barrett Browning's courtship and subsequent marriage to Robert Browning. The poems were originally personal and intended only for Robert Browning's eyes; subsequently, he persuaded Elizabeth Barrett Browning to publish them.

⇨ First impressions

1. Read the poem twice, the second time slowly, pausing after the fourth, eighth and last lines.

2. Write down your immediate impressions of who:
   - the speaking voice is
   - the poem is addressed to.

3. Select two of the following phrases which best describe the kind of love that is expressed in the poem:

unfulfilled love	*romantic love*	*sisterly love*	*passionate love*
one-way love	*unhappy love*	*broken love*	*distant love*

   Choose a phrase or line from the poem to justify your choices.

ℚ KEY VOCAB

insphere – encircle

Elizabeth Barrett Browning

⇨ Look a little closer

(1) On a copy of the poem, highlight in different colours all of the words and phrases that relate to:

- wild vines
- trees.

What does each image represent?
Explain why the poet decided to use these images.

(2) Because of the 'rules' followed by a sonnet writer, we can divide the poem into three sections. For each 'section' summarise the main ideas that the poet expresses, and select two quotations that conveys this clearly. The first has been started for you below.

Section	Main ideas	Key quotations
First quatrain (four lines) from: 'I think of thee! –' to 'hides the wood.'	*My thoughts of you, like a vine, grow and twist upwards*	'my thoughts do twine and bud'
Second quatrain from 'Yet,' to 'strong tree should,'		
Final 'sestet' of six lines from 'Rustle thy boughs' to 'too near thee.'		

⇨ Exploring the detail

(1) On a copy of the poem, highlight every instance of the word 'thee'.

- What does this tell us about the nature of the poet's thought processes?
- What is the effect of the continual use throughout the poem of words that rhyme with 'thee'?
- Think carefully about the line: 'I will not have my thoughts instead of thee'.

   How do you interpret what the poet is expressing about the relationship between what she thinks and what she wants?

(2) Return to the two extended metaphors of a vine and a tree, examples of which you have highlighted on a copy of the poem. Explore possible interpretations of what these metaphors reveal about the nature of romantic love between a woman and a man, as seen by the poet.

(3) Re-read the final three lines closely. The poet starts with 'Because' as she intends to convey a complex, elusive idea about why she **no longer** wants to think of her love. Write a paragraph to show your understanding of what she attempts to express.

(4) How might the **structure** of the poem reflect what it is that the poet wants to happen?

HINT

At the start of the poem the poet is not with her love … he is absent.

16

Tasks

1 In 'I think of thee!', the poet describes her 'deep joy'. Show, by making detailed reference to the form of the poem, and its use of imagery and rhythm, how the poet conveys a powerful sense of romantic love.

2 Write an analysis of the poem in which you explore how a Victorian and a twenty first century reader might have different views about the way that love is portrayed.

Key features

- Written in the classic sonnet form, made up of 14 lines in two groups of four, followed by two groups of three, with a regular rhyming pattern
- Repetition of key words and ideas
- Vivid imagery from the natural world

COMPARE WITH

- 'Love's Philosophy'
- 'Before You Were Mine'

Key themes

- How absence and anticipation can strengthen feelings of love
- The nature of the relationship between wife and husband
- Victorian attitudes to romantic love
- Is there a difference between female and male romantic love?

'Neutral Tones' by Thomas Hardy

The poem was written in 1867, following the death of Hardy's first wife, Emma.

⇨ First impressions

The choice of the title 'Neutral Tones' is an important part of the poem.

(1) What does the word 'neutral' suggest to you?

(2) 'Tone' has several meanings, as listed in the table below.

Read the whole poem through twice. How many of these aspects of the meaning of 'tone' can you identify? Pick out a word or phrase for each to illustrate your choice.

Meaning of 'tone'	Quotation
Sound of the voice – relating to pitch, quality and strength. How a voice expresses emotion, e.g. a 'lively tone', 'a sad tone'	
The 'mood' of a group, e.g. 'to raise the tone of a discussion'; 'to set the tone' with a joke or a serious comment	
The degree of colour, and of light and shade, in a picture or photograph	
Harmony between different colours, e.g. 'that carpet doesn't tone in with the wallpaper'	

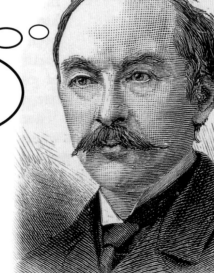

❝Since then, keen lessons that love deceives,
And wrings with wrong, have shaped to me
Your face❞

Thomas Hardy

(3) Of the following possible meanings of 'neutral', select **two** which now seem to you to best suit the way the idea is used in the poem.

- Disconnected
- Drained of colour
- Lifeless
- Neither positive or negative
- Standing aloof, indifferent, not engaged

For each, identify a phrase or line in the poem that justifies your choice.

⇨ Look a little closer

(1) Refer closely to the poem and copy and complete each of these short summaries of 'what seems to have happened' in the first **three** verses:

- The scenery on that day was …
- You looked at me but …
- We spoke but …
- You smiled but …

(2) Take each verse in turn. Read it through carefully and then invent your own 'subtitle' for the verse, which conveys what it is describing.

For example, one student decided to subtitle Verse 1 as 'Still life in winter'.

(3) The poem doesn't explicitly state the nature of the relationship, but hints at it. How do you interpret it? How long has it been in existence? What seems to have happened?

⇨ Exploring the detail

(1) On a copy of the poem, highlight all the words and phrases that convey a sense of **loss**, **rejection** and **death**. What does the use of these tell us about the way the poet views the relationship?

(2) How do you interpret each of the following lines?

- ✳ 'Over tedious riddles solved years ago;'
- ✳ 'The smile on your mouth was the deadest thing'
- ✳ 'Alive enough to have strength to die;'
- ✳ 'Like an ominous bird'
- ✳ 'keen lessons … have shaped to me'
- ✳ 'Your face,'

③ The form and structure of the poem have been carefully chosen to add to its meaning. Find examples where:

- the rhythm of a line captures a set of painful memories
- alliteration conveys bitterness
- the tense changes to show that a past event is still vivid and unalterable
- repetition of a description shows that the poet is trapped in his memories.

Tasks

1 Show how in 'Neutral Tones' Hardy creates the sense of a love that was once alive and beautiful, but has now failed. In your account, make sure that you:
- analyse the form and structure of the poem
- provide a detailed interpretation of how imagery and the sound of words are used to convey a sense of loss.

2 Explain why the title 'Neutral Tones' is so important to the rest of the poem. Make sure that you show how the title anticipates and sums up the way that the theme of love is treated in the poem.

Key features

- Written in a formal, tightly controlled structure – four verses each of four lines of iambic pentameter with a regular pattern or rhymes
- Repeated sets of images relating to the title of the poem
- Description of a scene, and memories of what passed, as if seen as a still life painting

Key themes

- Loss of love and the resulting sadness and bitterness
- The power of memory

COMPARE WITH

- Sonnet 29 –'I think of thee!'
- 'Winter Swans'

‘We caught her, fetched her home at last
And turned the key upon her, fast.’

‘The Farmer's Bride’ by Charlotte Mew

The poem was first published in 1916. It is in the form of a dramatic monologue.

⇨ First impressions

1. With the title of the poem in your mind, read the key quotation, above, which is taken from about halfway through the poem.

2. Based just on this fragment, speculate about the following questions:
   - Who was caught?
   - What might have happened?
   - What does the line about turning the key suggest about the attitude of the ‘We’?

3. Read Verse 1.
   - Whose voice is speaking in the poem?
   - Write a short paragraph of description of the speaker and what we know about his life and attitudes based on what he says and the way he speaks.
   - What is the speaker's explanation for why ‘she runned away’?

4. Read the whole poem. Write a second paragraph, adding to your description of the speaker, in which you comment on what else we learn about him, his marriage, and how he feels about the way things have turned out.

Charlotte Mew

⇨ Look a little closer

KEY VOCAB

fay – fairy or elf
leveret – young hare

1. Using a copy of the table below, trace the range of emotions expressed by the farmer as he relates his story. Select a quotation as evidence for each emotion. Look for evidence of feelings such as: sadness, yearning, anger, incomprehension, lack of feeling ('callousness'), admiration, surprise, frustration, pity.

Event	Farmer's emotions	Quotation
'Choosing' a bride	Need to make a quick choice, without much regard to emotion	'more's to do/At harvest-time than bide and woo.'
Wedding		
Searching for his wife		
Bringing her home		
The wife back at home		
Christmas time		
Present time		

2. The poem shows us what happened through the eyes of one character only. We never hear the wife's voice or her version of events. Use your detailed reading skills to trace what we know, and then what you can **infer**, about the farmer's wife, completing a copy of the table below:

Event	What we know	What can be inferred	Quotation
'Choosing' a bride	She was young	She was unprepared for marriage, perhaps had no choice	'Too young maybe –'
Wedding			'When us was wed she turned afraid'
Running away	She hid among the animals on the farm		
Brought back home		Suggestion that she is an 'outsider' in the rural community	
Her life back at home			

3. What aspects of the poem tell us that it was written about a time and place in the past?

22

⇨ Exploring the detail

① Investigate what the poem reveals about the farmer's attitude to his young wife, by analysing the way that the poem uses imagery.

- On a copy of the poem, highlight all the examples where the wife is described using a simile.
- What connects each of these images?
- What does this tell us about:
  - how the wife feels and reacts to her new life
  - the attitude that the farmer has towards his wife.

② The writer creates the persona of the farmer through her choice of language.

- Highlight four examples of non-standard English.
- What do these imply about the farmer and the kind of community he lives in?

③ Give your own interpretation of the effect of the following choice of words, commenting on what they suggest about the farmer and the wife he has 'taken':

✳ 'I **chose** a maid,'

✳ 'Like **the shut of a winter's day**/Her smile went out,'

✳ 'Should **properly** have been abed;'

✳ '"Not near, not near!" her eyes **beseech**/When one of **us** comes within **reach**.'

✳ '**One leaf** in the still air falls slowly down,'

✳ The highly charged repetition of '**down**', '**brown**', and '**hair**' in the final three lines.

④ Look closely at Verses 4 and 5. Each sets a different tone when compared to the rest of the poem.

- How would you describe the effect of the images used in Verse 4? What do they imply about the farmer's feelings about his bride?
- Explain how the choice of imagery in Verse 5 contributes to your understanding of the farmer's thoughts and feelings at this point in the poem.

Tasks

1 In the poem 'The Farmer's Bride' the farmer comments that ''Tis but a stair/Betwixt us.' What, in your view, does the poem reveal about what **really** separates the man and wife? Write a detailed answer, showing how the use of a dramatic monologue, the language choices and imagery of the poem present a picture of a failed marriage.

2 'It's impossible to know with whom Charlotte Mew most identifies – the strange young girl in the company of men, or the lonely farmer confused and pained by unrequited desire.'
Read these two differing interpretations of the poem, written at different times:

A farmer chooses a bride, but she isn't ready for marriage, and despite his love for her, she runs away. Although she returns, she behaves abnormally, and is lost to him. Sad and lonely, he admires her beauty but can't reach her. (1920s)

A farmer selects a bride, just like he'd choose to buy a farm animal. The marriage fails because he probably treats her badly, and she is frightened by their sexual relationship. When she returns having been 'caught', she is subdued and passive, living in fear for her life, treated like a pet, or a tamed animal: caged and confined. (2014)

Write a detailed commentary on the poem, giving your view on both of these interpretations, using evidence from the poem to support your views. Conclude by providing your own interpretation of the poem.

Key features

- A dramatic monologue, creating a distinctive speaking voice
- Imagery connected to the natural world
- Variety in tone in some verses

Key themes

- Unrequited love and unfulfilled desire
- The nature of marriage and why it fails
- The balance of power within a marriage, and how interpretations of this may change over time, from when a poem was written to how it is read now

COMPARE WITH
- 'Neutral Tones'
- 'Porphyria's Lover'

‘ love is proved in the letting go. ’

‘Walking Away’ by Cecil Day-Lewis

Day-Lewis once wrote about poetry: ‘We do not write in order to be understood; we write in order to understand.’

⇨ First impressions

1. Before you read the whole poem, reflect on what clues you get as to its main theme and ideas from these extracts:
   * *the title ‘Walking Away’*
   * *‘like a satellite/Wrenched from its orbit,’*
   * *‘That hesitant figure, eddying away/Like a winged seed’*
   * *‘nature’s give-and-take’*
   * *‘love is proved in the letting go.’*
   Whose thoughts might these be typical of?

2. Read the poem through, twice. Now answer these questions:
   * What incident is being remembered?
   * What impression do you form of the nature of the relationship being remembered?

⇨ Look a little closer

1. The phrase ‘Walking Away’ could indicate an attitude of **firmness** and **certainty**. Can you find examples from the poem that suggest otherwise?

2. Look closely at each verse in turn. Use these questions and prompts to explore what is being expressed in each.

Verse 1:
* Find two descriptions that suggest that change is in the air.
* What does the simile in lines 3 and 4 indicate about the nature of the relationship, and how the father feels about what's happening?

Verse 2:
* What does the image ‘half-fledged’ suggest?
* What does the description in lines 3 and 4 indicate about how the father imagines his son is also feeling?

Verse 3:
* What previous images does the phrase ‘eddying away’ connect to? What does the word ‘eddying’ convey?

🗨 KEY VOCAB

pathos – expressing pity or suffering

fledged – able to fly

irresolute – undecided or hesitant

25

Cecil Day-Lewis in study with elder son Nicholas

- Lines 3 and 4 of this verse are the start of the poet's attempt to express the main idea that he has written the poem, to 'try to understand'. Write a sentence in which you explain your thoughts on what the 'main idea' in the poem might be.

Verse 4:

- In the final verse the writer says that he has 'had worse partings'. What might it be about this particular parting that he finds so hard to deal with?
- Look closely at the concluding two lines. Explain what you think the poet is attempting to express about:

a) the meaning and nature of 'selfhood'

b) love between a parent and child. Think especially carefully about the use of the verb 'proved' which has at least three possible meanings: tested; shown to be genuine; made certain.

⇨ Exploring the detail

(1) The poet describes the son as a 'hesitant figure'. The poem also expresses hesitancy on behalf of the writer, however, as he reflects on that day, 18 years before. On a copy of the poem, highlight and label examples of each of the following:

- a sentence that is interrupted by a new thought
- a sentence that shows uncertainty
- a sentence that suggests that the writer is struggling to express something
- a verb that expresses a memory that won't go away, and continues to trouble the writer
- an adverb that suggests that the writer can only express an idea in an approximate way.

(2) There is one religious reference in the poem that, once understood, adds to the force of the main idea that is explored and expressed. In thinking about the 'parting', Day-Lewis writes that: 'it is roughly/ Saying what God alone could perfectly show'. This reference hints at what Christians believe about the relationship between God the father and Christ the son. The events related in the New Testament, summed up by: 'For God so loved the world, that he gave his only Son, that whoever believes in him should not perish but have eternal life.' (John 3:16).

- How does understanding the reference to this extract from the Bible add to the poem's meaning?

Task

1 'We do not write in order to be understood; we write in order to understand.'
Show by making close reference to the form and structure of the poem, and the poet's choice of language and use of various poetic devices, how this description is appropriate to 'Walking Away'.

Key features

- A formal structure: four verses, each with four lines, and with a regular rhyme scheme and rhythmical pattern to each line
- Imagery relating to the natural world
- Language and sentence patterns to convey the poet's state of mind

COMPARE WITH

- 'Mother, any distance'
- 'Letters from Yorkshire'

Key themes

- Nature
- Strength of parent–child love

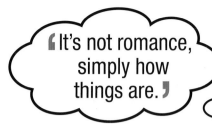

❝ It's not romance, simply how things are. ❞

Maura Dooley

'Letters from Yorkshire' by Maura Dooley

Maura Dooley was born in Cornwall, grew up in Bristol and, after working for some years in Yorkshire, now lives in London.

⇨ First impressions

1. Read Verse 1, and then pause:
   - Why might the arrival of the lapwings have prompted him to write a letter?

2. Read on to the end:
   - This poem appears in the 'Love and Relationships' cluster. How much of a love poem do you think this is? Where would you locate it on a scale of 1 to 10 where 1 is not really a love poem and 10 is definitely a love poem?

1	5	10

   - Pick out any lines or phrases that help you to make this initial judgement.

⇨ Look a little closer

(1) Part of the way the poem 'works' is through a set of comparisons between 'you' – the person in Yorkshire – and 'me' – the poet – and in particular the differences between their 'worlds'. Re-read the poem carefully, and copy and complete the table below, showing what the poem reveals about each person.

What we learn about 'you'	What we learn about 'me'
• Outdoors • Digging in his garden in Yorkshire in February • •	• Indoors • • • •

(2) Now sum up the main difference between the two people in a single sentence.

(3) The poem does not spell out the nature of the relationship but rather drops hints and suggestions. Use the following questions to work out for yourself what the two people might be thinking and feeling but not saying directly:

- What does the poet think about the life led by the letter writer?
- What might the poet feel about her own lifestyle?
- What wouldn't the letter writer 'say' in Verse 4?
- What does the use of the word 'souls' in the last line suggest to you about the nature of their relationship?

(4) Now read the poem again. Look at your initial judgement about the nature of the relationship being expressed. If the feelings explored are 'not romance' how would you sum up the relationship?

⇨ Exploring the detail

(1) Look in detail and offer your thoughts about the effect of some of the key **metaphors** in the poem. For example, one student wrote the following about the metaphor in Verse 1: 'his knuckles singing':

On one level this describes the feeling you get in your hands when you come into a warm room from the cold outdoors – your knuckles start to throb and burn. But 'singing' also suggests joyfulness and happiness, which I think is linked to seeing the lapwings.

Sound Barrier
POEMS 1982-2002
MAURA DOOLEY

② For each of the following, re-read the lines around the metaphor, and then explain what it suggests to you, and how it links to the effect of the poem as a whole:

✴ *'heartful of headlines'*

✴ *'feeding words onto a blank screen.'*

✴ *'pouring air and light into an envelope.'*

✴ *'our souls tap out messages'*

✴ *'across the icy miles.'*

③ Think carefully about these lines that offer an insight into the emotions that lie behind the surface of the poem. Give your interpretation of what you understand each to be saying:

✴ *'It's not romance, simply how things are.'*

✴ *'Is your life more real because you dig and sow?'*

✴ *'Still, it's you'*

✴ *'who sends me word of that other world'*

④ Look at the change in the pronouns used to describe the letter writer.

● Why might the poet have chosen to switch from using 'he' and 'his garden' in Verse 1, to the more personal 'you' at the end of Verse 2, and thereafter?

● What happens to the pronouns in the final line?

● How does this change add to what the poem suggests about the nature of the relationship?

Tasks

1 The poem is, in one sense, about the effect of words, of 'letters'. Think back over the poem and write three paragraphs in which you comment on:
  a) what the letter writer can do with words
  b) what the poet thinks about the words she is writing on screen
  c) how effectively the poet uses words to convey the nature of the relationship.

2 Show how, in 'Letters from Yorkshire', Maura Dooley creates a sense of both distance and closeness in a relationship. Comment on the ideas the poem explores; the use of contrast; and how the writer's choice of words and images add to the poem's effect.

Key features

● Five regular three-line verses

● Use of contrast

● Metaphors to create effects

● Combines descriptions of work and the exterior world with the interior world of thoughts and feelings

Key themes

● How a relationship can be both distant and close
● The importance of language in maintaining a close relationship

COMPARE WITH

■ Sonnet 29 – 'I think of thee!'

> ❝Crossing is not as hard as you might think.❞

'Eden Rock' by Charles Causley

Charles Causley was an only child whose father died when he was only seven. This is an autobiographical poem, although the actual event described might be at least partly imagined.

⇨ First impressions

1. Listen to Charles Causley reading the poem:
   www.poetryarchive.org/poem/eden-rock

2. Select two words from this list to describe the **tone** of the poem.

   conversational *personal* *dramatic*

   reflective *thoughtful* *mysterious*

   Find two lines from the poem to justify your choice.

⇨ Look a little closer

Explore this poem to develop your understanding of what the poet conveys about the thoughts and feelings he has about his parents.

1. Find examples of descriptions of both the father and mother that suggest that Causley:
   - feels respectful about his parents
   - is entranced by his mother's beauty
   - feels that his parents are somehow distant from him.

2. The poem, on one level, describes an ordinary event, remembered many years later. Identify **ordinary life** details from the poem, for example, the Thermos flask. Copy out the table below and add these ordinary life details to it from Verses 2 to 4.

💬 KEY VOCAB

sprigged – a traditional dress pattern, decorated with small design of flowered 'sprays'

Thermos – a type of vacuum flask for keeping liquids hot

31

(3) Another feature of this poem is how the poet captures **particular details** in a simple but vivid image. Select one example of this feature from each of Verses 2 to 4 and add them to the table.

Verse	Ordinary life details	Vivid image of a specific detail
1	'Suit/Of Genuine Irish Tweed'	'terrier Jack … trembling at his feet.'
2		
3		
4		

⇨ Exploring the detail

The poem is **more** than just a description of an ordinary event, remembered many years later.

(1) Here are some examples from the poem where there is a suggestion of the **extraordinary** in the ordinary, or a hint of something **strange**, **marvellous** or **mysterious** alongside the everyday. Copy and complete the table below to add your thoughts and responses about what is suggested. Think about what connotations the words have for you, or what other ideas might be suggested.

Verse	Extraordinary or mysterious aspect	Your thoughts
Title	'Eden Rock'	Suggests a place of innocence, or of beauty and peace
1	'somewhere beyond'	
2	'Her hair … takes on the light'	
4	'as if lit by three suns' 'drifted stream'	
5	'They beckon to me from the other bank.' 'stream-path'	

(2) Most of the poem is written in the present tense. What is the effect of this?

(3) Look closely at Verse 5.

    a) Why might the poet have decided to separate the final line from the previous three?

    b) This is the only line in the poem written in the past tense. What is the effect of this?

(4) Find examples where the rhythm of the poem slows, or is interrupted, to create a sense of a scene unfolding in slow motion, or in an unhurried, almost dream-like way.

⑤ The poem deliberately makes reference to words and phrases that are often thought to have some kind of **symbolic** meaning. Here are some examples:

- Eden: possibly a biblical reference to the Garden of Eden – the place of first **innocence**. As a name, Eden means **delight**.
- Streams, rivers and in particular the idea of crossing a river: possibly symbolising a spiritual journey, or a journey to the 'promised land'; in Greek mythology, the River Styx was seen as dividing the earth from the afterlife, the living from the dead. Water itself may symbolise **purity**, or **change**.

How does knowing about the possible symbolic meaning of these ideas add to your understanding of how the poem can be seen as more than just a vivid description of a childhood memory?

Tasks

The 'meaning' of this poem can't be summarised, or reduced to a single interpretation. It is deliberately elusive and, for many readers, changes slightly every time the poem is read. As a reader, you have to respond to both the words on the page, the images that are created and the hints and suggestions that the poem creates for you.

Here are three interpretations from students who have studied and thought carefully and imaginatively about the poem:

For me, 'Eden Rock' symbolises how the poet sees his parents, after their death, calling to him to join them.

I think that the poet is referring to how his parents aged 25 and 23 were 'calling' or 'beckoning' to him to join them in their lives – so in a way it's like them waiting for the unborn child to join them in their lives.

The poem suggests to me a time of lost innocence and simplicity that the poet wishes he could recapture but knows that he can't.

Re-read the poem with each interpretation in mind.

Decide:

1 Is there one of these interpretations that is closest to the way you interpret the poem? If so, copy it out and use it as the first sentence of a paragraph in which you explain how you interpret the poem in this way.
2 Is it possible for all three interpretations to be justified? Write a detailed paragraph explaining your view.
3 Do you have a different way of interpreting the poem? Write a paragraph in which you explain your thoughts.

Make detailed reference to the poem to justify your opinions.

Key features

- Traditional form, four-line verses, ABAB rhyme scheme, regular metre
- Ordinary details, clear description, simple diction (words)
- Conversational, personal, autobiographical tone
- Use of the present tense to create sense of immediacy
- Reference to symbols that may denote death, being born, innocence and purity

COMPARE WITH

- 'Before You Were Mine'
- 'Mother, Any Distance'
- 'Walking Away'

'Follower' by Seamus Heaney

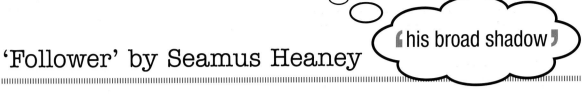

(his broad shadow)

This poem explores the changing relationship between a father and son, as seen through the son's eyes.

⇨ First impressions

(1) Write down the word 'follower' and then make a list of other words and phrases that it suggests to you as you read the poem through.

(2) Which of the words or phrases that you wrote down are closest to your first impressions of how the idea of a 'follower' is explored in the poem?

KEY VOCAB

wing – a part of a plough blade that can be adjusted to enable the soil to be cut and loosened effectively

sock – the part of the plough blade that slices through the soil

sod – a lump of turf or earth

headrig – the point in the corner of a field where the ploughing team have to turn through 180 degrees

furrow – the narrow groove made in soil by a plough blade; a ship's track through the sea

⇨ Look a little closer

(1) In the first three verses the poem captures the young son's admiration for the expertise and skill of his ploughman father. Copy the table below and add to the list of the qualities that the son most admires. For each, choose a short quotation to illustrate it.

Quality	Quotation
Power	'shoulders globed like a full sail'
Precision	
Command	

(2) In Verses 4 and 5 and the first two lines of Verse 6, we see the contrast between father and son.

    a) Select three images from the poem that convey a sense of the power and size of the father. Choose one and write a paragraph that explains how the image works and its effect on the reader.

    b) Find five **verbs** used in the poem that relate to the son. Explain how these are the opposite of the description of the father.

⇨ Exploring the detail

(1) A feature of the poem is how the father and son are portrayed through sets of extended or developed metaphors. Make three collections:

    a) Images connected with ships, sailing and the sea. What do they add to the sense of the way the father is described?

    b) A collection of words and phrases that suggest 'expertise'; for example, 'set', 'fit'.

    c) Words that are connected to 'nuisance'.

(2) Look closely at the way the poem conveys sounds by using alliteration and assonance. Here is one set of words that are connected by sound:

clicking

fit

sock

headrig

breaking

pluck

back

wake

These words mostly contain short vowels, with a distinctive 'click' made' by the /ck/ consonant. These are like some of the sounds made by the father working with the horses and plough, they also provide a pattern of sounds which run through the poem. Done well, this is a sign of an expert writer at work, adjusting his words and fine-tuning his poem so that it is strong and sturdy.

Find and mark on a copy of the poem another set of sound patterns which use the long vowels /o/ (as in 'furr**ow**') and /ow/ as in 'pl**ough**'. What idea connects all of the words that you have collected?

(3) Here is an example of another poetic technique – called **enjambment** – where the sense of a line runs on into the next, to add emphasis, or convey an action:

> 'like a full sail strung
> Between the shafts'

④ By using enjambment, the poet spreads the description of the sail across two lines – just how a sail is strung between two shafts. Find two more examples of this technique, and for each, explain how it adds to the meaning of the poem.

⑤ Focus in on the last three lines of the poem. Heaney uses a **caesura** (a sudden break in the metre or rhythm of a line) to make the sudden change from 'then' to 'now', signalled by the final sentence beginning 'But'.

- What happens to the tense of the verbs compared to the rest of the poem?
- Explain in what ways the poem shows a reversal of roles in the last two and a half lines.
- Give your interpretation of the last line of the poem. There is a **literal** interpretation of how the father now 'follows' the son, but the poem suggests other ways as well. In what ways might the poet feel that his father 'will not go away'?

Tasks

You should use your knowledge and understanding of the poem to provide a detailed written answer, and use quotations from the poem to provide evidence for your views.

1 What does the poem show of the relationship of father and son, and how time has changed this?

2 'This is a poem about expertise and precision.' Show how this statement is true both for ploughing and for poetry.

Key features

- Six quatrains, each with four lines, and with a regular pattern of rhyme ABAB
- Use of past and present tense to contrast 'then' and 'now'
- Repeated sounds and words that echo through the poem
- The poet's admiration for his father's expertise

COMPARE WITH

- 'Eden Rock'
- 'Mother, Any Distance'
- 'Before You Were Mine'

Key theme

- The idea that time changes relationships

'**Anchor. Kite.**'

Simon Armitage

'Mother, any distance' by Simon Armitage

First impressions

1. Read the poem once, silently to yourself.

2. Now read it again, out loud this time. Try to get a sense of the music of the words. Some lines will be read quickly, with the rhythm of ordinary speech. Other lines will suggest a slower rhythm, or an interrupted one. Some will hint at an internal rhyme.

3. What situation is the poem literally about? What does the son need help with?

4. Note down any immediate ideas you have about the poem. Continue this list of words and ideas:

Leaving or moving away ...
Always there ...

Look a little closer

1. Read the poem for a third time. Look at the way that Simon Armitage describes himself. What do the following images suggest to you?

> - 'reporting ... back to base,'
> - 'the line still feeding out,'
> - 'I space-walk'

38

(2) Look more closely at the way that the poem explores the relationship between son and mother, verse by verse. For each verse, comment first on the literal meaning and then your interpretation of what the choice of words and images suggests about the relationship. An example has been given for Verse 1.

Verse	Literal meaning	Interpreted meaning	Key quotation
Verse 1 (first quatrain)	Mother helps son to measure up for a new home	He is moving out of home for the first time? He feels a bit daunted by the experience.	'the acres of the walls, the prairies of the floors.'
Verse 2 (second quatrain)			
Verse 3 (sestet)			

(3) Return to the title – which is lifted from the opening three words of the poem. Explain how, as a title, it suggests more than its literal use in the first quatrain.

⇨ Exploring the detail

(1) The poem expresses and explores the relationship between child (in this case a grown-up child) and parent. Collect two sets of images:
- those that suggest moving away, leaving
- those that stress connection, bonds and ties.

(2) Look at the first word of each verse. How does the shift from: 'Mother' to 'You', to 'I' add to the main theme of the poem?

(3) Focus in on lines 7 and 8:

> 'the line still feeding out, unreeling
> years between us. Anchor. Kite.'

Focus in on lines 12 and 13:

> 'two floors below your fingertips still pinch,
> the last one-hundredth of an inch … I reach'

- Think carefully about what each of the highlighted words and phrases suggest, and also how each relates to the overall theme of the poem – the nature of the relationship between mother and son.
- For each, write a sentence in which you explain why this particular, precise selection of words is effective.

4 Focus in on the last two lines. Taken literally, the 'hatch' is probably a roof skylight, perhaps in an attic room. But, by now, the poem is about much more than a description of the completion of a household task (i.e. measuring). Read back through the whole poem.

- What is your interpretation of other meanings of what the writer is 'reaching' towards?
- Why might the sky be described as 'endless'?
- What is your interpretation of 'to fall or fly'?

5 Simon Armitage has spoken about how he chooses the **form** of a poem once he has started to collect words, images and lines, which then suggest to him how a poem might be structured. The form of this poem is based on a **sonnet**. However, it doesn't follow a strict pattern, but instead manipulates the form for effect. In the poem, find examples of:

- one line running into the next, and almost 'acting' out the meaning
- a long 'run on' sentence
- single-word sentences
- short lines.

For each, explain in detail how the choice of words, and use of poetic technique, work to convey meaning, and suggest something important about the relationship that the poem deals with.

Tasks

1 Show, by writing a detailed commentary on the poem, how 'Mother, any distance' uses an extended metaphor to explore the nature of a parent–child relationship.

2 The sonnet form was traditionally used to express ideas about love in its many varieties. Show how Simon Armitage imaginatively uses the sonnet form to offer a personal view on love.

Key features

- Loose sonnet form, with two quatrains and a sestet with a tailpiece – or additional final line
- The whole poem is an extended metaphor
- Connected imagery to express the way a relationship can be both constant and change

Key themes

- Parent–child relationship, and how this develops and changes over time
- Love as 'letting go'

COMPARE WITH

- 'Walking Away'
- 'Before You Were Mine'
- 'Follower'

❝I'm not here yet. The thought of me doesn't occur in the ballroom with the thousand eyes …❞

'Before You Were Mine' by Carol Ann Duffy

This is an autobiographical poem, based on memories, photographs and stories heard.

⇨ First impressions

① Think about the title of the poem. What does it suggest to you about the kind of relationship that the poem will explore?

One student wrote:

It sounds like the title of a pop song, a love song, possibly from boy to girl?

② Read Verse 1. Look for clues:
- What age might the three girls be?
- What period do you associate with the 'polka-dot dress'?

③ Re-read the first line. Who might be 'ten years away'? And who might the 'you' be that the title and verse refer to?

④ Now read the rest of the poem. As you read, think about questions 2 and 3 above. What additional ideas do you begin to gather about who is the speaking voice? And who is being described?

⇨ Look a little closer

Carol Ann Duffy explains that the poem 'is essentially a kind of love poem addressed to my mother'. The poem came about as a result of looking at old photographs of her mother, and remembering the stories her mother used to tell of the time before she had children.

The poem offers two perspectives:

- The poet remembering and imagining what her mother's life was like in the decade before she had children.
- The poet remembering and imagining what she herself felt, and still feels, about that life.

(1) On a copy of the poem, highlight specific images in each verse that present a picture of the mother as a teenager. Annotate each with a summary of what it shows. For example, here are a student's annotations for Verse 1:

🗩 KEY VOCAB

a thousand eyes – 'The Night Has a Thousand Eyes' was a popular song first recorded by American singer Bobby Vee which reached number 3 in the UK charts in March 1963

close – a Scottish word for the entry to a tenement building or block of flats

George Square and Portobello – references to places in Scotland

I'm ten years away from the corner you laugh on
Mother happy, carefree? ⟩

with your pals, Maggie McGeeney and Jean Duff.
↖ *Probably a photo*

The three of you bend from the waist, holding
each other, or your knees, and shriek at the pavement.
Present tense used ⟩

Your polka-dot dress blows round your legs. Marilyn.
↖ *1950s*   ↗

Image of Marilyn Monroe

(2) Here is a selection of lines which reveal what Carol Ann Duffy felt, and still feels about her mother's previous life. Explain what these descriptions reveal about how the child felt about her mother.

✳ 'I knew you would dance/ like that.'

✳ 'I remember my hands in those high-heeled red shoes,'

✳ 'Cha cha cha! You'd teach me the steps'

✳ 'Even then/I wanted the bold girl winking in Portobello,'

⇨ Exploring the detail

(1) The final line of the poem describes 'where you sparkle and waltz and laugh'.

Find two images in the poem for each of the following:
- Bright lights
- Dancing
- Laughter

For each, write a sentence explaining what the image conveys or suggests to you.

(2) 'I see you, clear as scent.' Explain why this image is such a powerful one:

- in capturing something important about the mother
- as a way of describing how the poem as a whole works.

(3) Look closely at the language and diction. The tone is **conversational**, at times very **intimate**.

- Write a paragraph in which you comment in detail on this aspect of the poem, using a few carefully chosen quotations to illustrate the points that you make.
- Write a second paragraph in which you explain the overall effect of this choice of language, and what it conveys of the nature of the love that the daughter feels for her mother.

(4) Re-read the poem. Focus on the areas highlighted below, explaining your response to each in detail:

- What do the first line of Verses 1–3 suggest about the difference between the life her mother imagined for herself, and the one she eventually 'found'?
- In Verse 4, what, specifically, does the choice of the word 'wrong' in the description of her mother dancing on 'the **wrong** pavement' suggest?
- What does the choice of the adjective 'glamorous' in the phrase 'That **glamorous love** lasts' suggest about the poet's view of the love she felt for her mother? How does this word connect to many of the other images in the poem?
- Finally, revisit the title. Write a paragraph in which you explain how the words 'before' and 'you were mine' are reflected in what the poem has to say about the way someone's life changes when they have children.

Tasks

1 'This is a poem written from the perspective of a child who is fiercely imagining the impossible – the living image of the mother pre-motherhood.'

Show how Carol Ann Duffy recreates in words a time before she was born. Comment in detail on:
- the effect of the imagery in the poem
- how its structure and language combine to bring to life her mother's world.

2 Write your own appreciation of the poem, showing how you respond to the language, and explain in detail what you understand about the way that the poem treats the theme of love.

One student wrote:

This poem is full of love, but I also can detect some sadness in it as well.

3 Show how the poem uses language and imagery relating to 'glamorous love' to present a picture of a child's love for her mother.

Key features

- The poem is structured in four regular verses, but without a rhyme scheme or a regular metre
- Conversational, intimate tone
- Inversion of the usual way that a child–mother relationship is described

Key themes

- The complex nature of love between a child and a parent
- Love felt by a child for the imagined glamorous life led by her mother before she appeared on the scene

COMPARE WITH
- 'Walking Away'
- 'Mother, Any Distance'

'until the swans came and stopped us with a show of tipping in unison.'

'Winter Swans' by Owen Sheers

This poem is from the collection *Skirrid Hill*, published in 2005. 'Skirrid' is derived from the Welsh word *Ysgirid* meaning divorce or separation.

⇨ First impressions

(1) Before reading the poem, think about the attributes of swans. What are they often seen as being representative of?

(2) The poem is, in one sense, a straightforward account of a moment in time.

- Read the poem twice, once silently, the second time aloud. As you read, allow the rhythm of the words to emerge. Think about the situation that the poem describes.
- Write, in prose, a short summary of the simple story that the poem tells. You might, for example, start like this:

A couple, possibly lovers, are walking beside a lake. The weather is …

⇨ Look a little closer

1. Re-read Verses 1 and 2. Explain how the poem uses the weather as a way of showing what is going on between the two people.

2. Read Verses 3 and 4 again. Look closely at how the swans are described. Explain what it is about the swans that 'stops' the two as they walk. What specifically is it about the way that the swans behave that is striking and grabs their attention?

3. Read the last three verses again.
   - Why might the speaker in the poem have not replied to the comment 'They mate for life'?
   - Pick out the words that show that the hand-holding was a surprise.
   - If the poem opens in rough weather, how would you describe the mood or atmosphere at the end? What words and phrases lead you to this conclusion?

⇨ Exploring the detail

1. Explore the way in which each of the following descriptions of the natural world can also have a meaning related to the couple's relationship. For each, write a sentence in which you offer your interpretation:
   - ✳ *'clouds had given their all'*
   - ✳ *'waterlogged earth'*
   - ✳ *'gulping for breath'*
   - ✳ *'skirted the lake,'* (think about the idea of 'skirting' round deep water)
   - ✳ *'boats righting in rough weather'*
   - ✳ *'stilling water'*
   - ✳ *'settling after flight'*

2. A feature of the poem is the way that the writer uses a range of connected imagery to show how the swans are different to the human couple. For each of these images, explain what it implies about the swans:
   - ✳ *'tipping in unison.'*
   - ✳ *'As if rolling weight down their bodies to their heads'*
   - ✳ *'halved themselves in the dark water,'*
   - ✳ *'icebergs of white feather,'*
   - ✳ *'boats righting in rough weather'*
   - ✳ *'porcelain over the stilling water'*

③ Read the first line of verse 6 aloud. Explain how the writer almost creates the sensation that is described through his choice of words, sounds and the rhythm or 'beat' of the line.

④ Focus on the last four lines. Look carefully, and then explain in detail how the poet brings together the two contrasting sets of images that have been used through the poem, to show the change in the relationship by the end.

- What is the effect of the metaphor describing the hands as 'swimming' together?
- How effective do you consider the final simile to be? Explain how it is an appropriate conclusion to the poem.
- The writer chose to alter the structure of the poem at the end, separating the final two lines out. Explain how this contributes to the action that concludes the poem.

Tasks

1 Show how, in 'Winter Swans', Owen Sheers creates the sense of a significant change in a relationship. Explain how the poet uses a set of connected images to convey the change in mood and tone.
2 Write an analysis of the poem that shows how the poet uses references and images from the natural world to capture a significant moment in a human relationship. Conclude your analysis by offering a personal opinion and reflection on the poem as a whole. How effective do you find it as a depiction of 'love renewed'?

Key features

- Formal structure: three-line verses, with a final shorter two-line verse
- Images of nature used to convey ideas about a relationship
- The poem describes a moment in time, written from one person's point of view

COMPARE WITH
- 'Neutral Tones'

Key theme

- Reconciliation and the possibility of renewal in a relationship

Hey Singh, ver yoo bin?

Daljit Nagra

'Singh Song!' by Daljit Nagra

Daljit Nagra is a second-generation British Asian who grew up in West London and Sheffield – where his parents owned a corner shop. His poems are a playful mix of English, Punjabi and Punjabi-accented English.

⇨ First impressions

(1) What does the use of a pun (sing/Singh) in the title suggest to you about the subject matter and the style and tone of the poem?

(2) The poem is written as a dramatic monologue, in which the writer creates a character and a distinctive speaking voice.

Watch a video clip of Daljit Nagra reading the poem:

www.bbc.co.uk/learningzone/clips/daljit-nagra-singh-song-poem-only/12251.html

Make a list of the features of the poem that are directly related to the idea of it being a 'song'.

⇨ Look a little closer

(1) What **information** does the poem provide about the main speaker, the shopkeeper 'Singh'? Make a list, starting with:

Works for his father who owns a chain of shops
Newly married

KEY VOCAB

Putney – a place on the banks of the River Thames, but also a Punjabi word meaning 'wife'

(2) It is probable that Singh's new wife is the result of an arranged marriage. Investigate what kind of bride she is – traditional or rebellious.

- On a copy of the poem, highlight any details that suggest that Singh's wife is behaving in a traditional way.
- In a different colour, highlight any details that suggest that she doesn't conform to a traditional role.
- For each of these details that describe Singh's wife, write a sentence to explain what it suggests about her:

✳ 'high heel tap'

✳ 'her Sikh lover site'

✳ 'tiny eyes ov a gun'

✳ 'she wear a Tartan sari'

(3) The 'chorus' sections (in italics) show that the customers are critical of Singh's shop. However, he doesn't answer them. What does his lack of response, and what he goes on to talk about, suggest to you about Singh's attitude?

⇨ Exploring the detail

(1) Analyse the way that the poem creates a distinctive speaking voice by deliberately using a form of non-standard English.

On a copy of the poem, highlight examples of:

- English words that are spelt phonetically to imitate English spoken with a Punjabi accent
- non-standard grammar
- changes to regular English word order (e.g. 'he vunt me not to')
- invented or altered words or phrases
- missing words (e.g. 'ven nobody in')
- non-standard verb forms
- phrases used by the speaker that make him sound comical.

② Re-read the section from 'Late in de midnight hour' to the end of the poem.

- Explain the effect of each of these images:
- ✳ 'di precinct is **concrete-cool**'
- ✳ 'vee cum down **whispering stairs**'
- The couple are described looking out through the front window of the shop, staring past signs and posters at the moon. Explain what the poem might be suggesting here about their relationship.
- Why might the poem end with a conversation about how much things cost (the moon, his wife)?

③ Asked to suggest what the poem has to say about love and relationships, two students wrote:

Love is more important than business and earning money.
The younger generation always rebel against their parents,
and British Asians are no different.

- What is your view?
- Write a paragraph in which you give your interpretation of what the poem has to say about this theme. Use quotations accompanied by a commentary as evidence for your conclusions.

Tasks

1 Show, by referring in detail to the poem, how Daljit Nagra creates a distinctive character through voice in the 'Singh Song!'
2 Explain how, through the creation of character, use of humour and playing around with the English language, the poem 'Singh Song!' explores some important ideas about love and relationships.

Key features

- The poem is a dramatic monologue (with a chorus), creating a character through the way he uses language
- In form, the poem is loosely based on the structure of songs, using rhyme and repeated words and phrases
- Word play – puns, invented spellings; non-standard dialect

Key themes

- Romantic love contrasted with the need to earn a living
- Differences between the generations

COMPARE WITH
- 'The Farmer's Bride'
- 'Porphyria's Lover'

❛the slow pulse of his good heart.❜

'Climbing My Grandfather' by Andrew Waterhouse

⇨ First impressions

①Read the poem twice, the second time slowly.

- What impression do you gain of the 'grandfather' from the way he is described in the poem? Choose three phrases that help to create this impression.
- What impression do you form of what the speaker thinks and feels about his or her grandfather?
- Think about the title and what the poem describes. The poem is an **extended metaphor**. Explain the comparison between the two different things that runs through the whole poem.

⇨ Look a little closer

①The poem is an imagined journey, using the language of climbing to convey the closeness a child feels for his or her grandfather.

- On a copy of the poem, highlight all of the phrases that relate directly to climbing. For example: 'do it free, without a rope or net.'
- In a different colour, highlight where each stage in the climb occurs. This is often signalled by words such as 'By', 'At' and 'then'.
- Number each stage of the climb – you should be able to identify ten stages. The first two are:

✸ Up onto the shoes ('brogues')

✸ Climbing the trousers

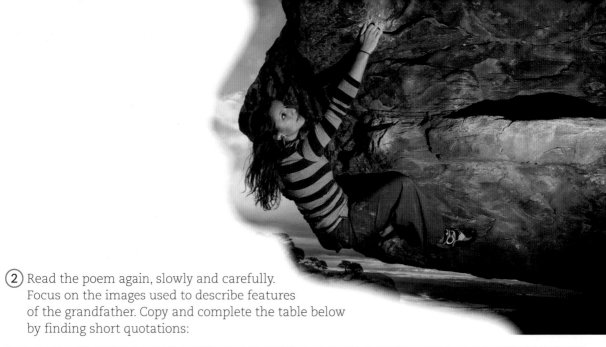

2. Read the poem again, slowly and carefully.
Focus on the images used to describe features
of the grandfather. Copy and complete the table below
by finding short quotations:

Images of age and experience	Images of strength and solidity	Images that convey respect and love
'old brogues, dusty and cracked;'	'overhanging shirt'	'like warm ice.'

⇨ Exploring the detail

1. The poem is full of images that **combine** the **human** and the **geographical**. Read this example, with a commentary by a student:

'By the overhanging shirt': his shirt is overhanging because he probably has a full belly, so it overhangs his trousers. But an 'overhang' is also a description of a rock feature, which can be hard or even impossible to climb.

2. Write your own commentary for examples of this technique. Start with 'earth-stained hand' – and then identify four other examples.

3. The form of the poem is an important element in its overall effect. Why do you think Andrew Waterhouse decided to use the structure of one single extended verse with a regular line length?

4. The poem concludes with a description of a heart beating. Explain how the way that the last line is written conveys the idea of a heart beating.

Task

1 Show how Andrew Waterhouse creates a vivid picture of a child's love and respect for his grandfather through his imaginative use of language.

Key features

- The poem is an example of an extended metaphor
- Images from rock climbing are combined with descriptions of an old person
- The form and structure add to its overall effect

COMPARE WITH

- 'Follower'
- 'Mother, Any Distance'

Key theme

- A child's perspective on the love and respect for an older relative

Writing a comparison answer

Here are two examples of a comparison question in the GCSE examination.

Read each question carefully. What, exactly, are you being asked to do? Underline the key instruction words in each of these questions.

1. Compare how relationships between parents and children are presented in 'Mother, Any Distance' and one other poem from 'Love and Relationships'.

2. Compare the ways that poets present views and ideas about love that has failed in 'Neutral Tones' and one other poem from 'Love and Relationships'.

When you answer a comparison question you need to:
1 Compare two poems:
   - One poem will be chosen for you and printed in the examination paper.
   - Select a second poem to use for your comparison. It needs to be an appropriate one.
   - Discuss the **similarities** and **differences** between the two poems.
2 Analyse and explain how an idea, an attitude or a theme is presented or expressed:
3 Show your understanding of the **methods** used in each poem:
   - **structure** – its form and how this contributes to its meaning and effect
   - **word choices** and **poetic techniques** to convey effects and add to the meaning
   - **tone**, or **attitude** – the way that the poem shows how the poet (or perhaps a character or speaking voice in the poem) thinks and feels.
4 Express **your personal view and interpretation** of what each poem is saying or implying about the theme or ideas.

How to write a good answer to a comparison question

(1) Prepare your answer

Use and adapt a planning grid like the one below so that you can decide what to include in your answer.

Focus of the question: e.g. how relationships between parents and children are presented	
Poem 1	**Poem 2**
Similarities	
Ideas/theme Form and structure Word choices and poetic techniques Tone and attitude	Ideas/theme Form and structure Word choices and poetic techniques Tone and attitude
Differences	
Ideas/theme Form and structure Word choices and poetic techniques Tone and attitude	Ideas/theme Form and structure Word choices and poetic techniques Tone and attitude

(2) Plan your essay

Sort out what your main points are going to be and how you will organise your ideas using the following:

- A short opening paragraph: explain which poems you will write about (titles and poets), and give an initial outline of the main points of comparison you intend to make. Show that you are setting out to write in a comparative way.
- At least three main paragraphs where you ensure that you write about both poems, cross-referencing ideas. Refer to the poems in detail, commenting, analysing and interpreting. Select some key quotations that you will use as examples.
- A conclusion where you provide your personal views or original ideas and sum up what you have concluded about the two poems.

You will need to learn how to prepare and plan an answer quickly, in examination conditions. To start with you will probably take a longer time than will be available in the examination, but this is a skill to improve through practice.

(3) Stitch your ideas together

A good comparison essay is one that has lots of good ideas that 'cohere' (fit together) so that your thinking is made clear to the reader. To do this, as you write, use a range of **cohesive devices** – words and phrases that link or connect your ideas up. Some of these will be within a paragraph, while others will link across sentences or even paragraphs, for example:

Although Poem X shows how ... in Poem Y the writer ...

In contrast to ... or because of this ....

Cohesive words and phrases	
Add	also, furthermore, moreover, and, for example, especially
Contrast	however, nevertheless, on the other hand, but, instead, in contrast, yet, though, at least, in fact, by comparison
Concede	although, nevertheless
Reinforce	besides, anyway, after all
Explain	for example, in other words
Sequence	first, first of all, then, next, finally
Indicate cause and effect	and so, because, since, so, consequently, as a result, thanks to this, because of this, thus

(4) Use appropriate terminology

As you have worked on the poems in this book, you have encountered, understood and used a wide range of useful terms to describe exactly what a writer has done to make a poem 'work' and have an effect on the reader. In a comparison essay, when you write about the **way** that a poet presents ideas, or the **methods** used to express a view, you should describe their techniques and methods by using the appropriate terminology.

Caution: only use a term if it is linked to a point you are making about the effect of the technique or approach. You get no marks for simply spotting techniques.

(5) Provide an evaluative response

Don't just describe, explain or comment. Make sure that you also write about your **appreciation** of a poem's qualities, and your **interpretation** of what a poem seems to you to be striving to express.

Remember: most poems, especially good ones, can't be reduced to a summary; they don't communicate a single meaning. Poems are full of concentrated language; they often hint and suggest at ideas and feelings that aren't immediately obvious. Cecil Day-Lewis, who was Poet Laureate from 1968 to 1972, said this: 'We do not write in order to be understood; we write in order to understand.'

As a reader you bring your experience and ideas **to** a poem. A good comparison essay should show that you have thought about the poem, have **concentrated** your attention on it, and have developed your views, your interpretation. To achieve a higher level, you should show that you can see different possible interpretations, rather than settling for just one.

Tasks

1 For each of the two questions on page 54, practise the two initial stages – preparation and planning – before writing your essay. Use the formats provided on pages 54–57.

2 Read this example of a student's opening paragraph for Question 1.

Question 1: Compare how relationships between parents and children are presented in 'Mother, Any Distance' and one other poem from 'Love and Relationships'.

Relationships between parents and children feature in a number of the poems in the Anthology. Simon Armitage's 'Mother, any distance' is written from the perspective of a grown-up son reflecting on how he needs to grow away from his mother, whilst recognising that she is 'always there' for him. In contrast, in 'Walking Away', Cecil Day-Lewis describes his reactions as his son (who is perhaps aged nine or ten) walks away from him after a school football game. Although both poems deal with the way children have to grow away from their parents, and also both write about ordinary incidents (a football match; measuring up a house for furnishings), each presents a quite different perspective.

3 Annotate a copy of the paragraph above to show:
  - an outline of the main point of comparison between the two poems
  - two examples of cohesive words and phrases that connect up ideas
  - an example of a similarity
  - an example of a difference.

4 Write your **opening paragraph** for Question 2. Focus on setting a **comparative tone**, explaining the poems you have chosen, and outlining the main ideas that you will explore in the rest of the essay.

5 For either Question 1 (using the opening paragraph above), or 2, now write the rest of your comparative essay.

6 **Selecting which poems to use in comparison**
Copy and complete the table on page 58. You can either work on this as you work with the poems, or after you have completed this work, as a way of revising and summarising. Use categories from this list or add your own.
  - marriage
  - romantic love
  - parent and child
  - love and loss
  - destructive love
  - distant relationships
  - desire
  - families

You should note that some poems may cover more than one category.

Poem	Aspect(s) of the theme presented	Additional comments including method and form
'When We Two Parted'	Love and loss	
'Love's Philosophy'	Desire	
'Porphyria's Lover'		Dramatic monologue
Sonnet 29 – 'I think of thee!'		Sonnet
'Neutral Tones'		
'The Farmer's Bride'	Marriage; destructive love	
'Walking Away'		
'Letters from Yorkshire'		
'Eden Rock'		
'Follower'	Parent and child	
'Mother, Any Distance'		
'Before You Were Mine'		
'Winter Swans'		
'Singh Song!'		Dramatic monologue; playful use of language
'Climbing My Grandfather'	Families	

❛Look on my works, ye Mighty, and despair!❜

'Ozymandias' by Percy Bysshe Shelley

⇨ First impressions

Shelley wrote the poem 'Ozymandias' in 1818. Most think it refers to a statue of the powerful Egyptian ruler Ramesses II, the head of whom is pictured above and which was brought to London at about that time.

The poem, on one level, recounts a story told by an explorer or traveller who has returned from an expedition to a remote desert. Read the poem and then copy and complete the description below:

The traveller found the remains of …

All that was left was … and …

On closer inspection he saw an inscription which read: '…'

The statue's remains were surrounded by …

⇨ Look a little closer

① 'Ozymandias' is written as a **sonnet**. This is a traditional verse form, made up of 14 lines with a strict rhyme scheme and structure. Shelley was innovative in his use of the sonnet form and invented his own rhyme scheme, as seen in this poem.

Read the poem aloud two or three times. Listen to the sound of the words. See if you can pick up the rhythm of each line, and also the unusual rhyme scheme.

② There are four people mentioned in the poem:

    a) The poet/narrator (the 'I' in the first line).
    b) The traveller who describes what he saw.
    c) Ozymandias, 'king of kings'.
    d) The sculptor who fashioned the great statue.

    What facts do we learn about each of these from the poem?

③ Look closely at the three lines (6, 7, 8) that describe the sculptor's achievements. What is it that the sculptor has managed to do?

④ One way of thinking about the **structure** of the poem is to think about how the traveller's description changes **focus**. Notice how the traveller firstly describes the 'Two vast and trunkless legs' as if he is seeing them from a distance. Copy and complete the analysis:

Description	Focus
'Two vast and trunkless legs'	Distance view
'shatter'd visage'	
'wrinkled lip and sneer'	
'on the pedestal these words appear:'	
'The lone and level sands'	

⑤ Explain how this use of different perspectives contributes to the ideas that the poem explores about **power and greatness**.

⇨ Exploring the detail

① Focus on the descriptions of the head that lies separated from its body on the sand. For each of the words and phrases that describe the way the head appears to the traveller, consider what each suggests to you (the first has been completed for you):

KEY VOCAB

trunkless – without a head or body

visage – face

mock'd – there are two possible meanings: 'ridiculed'; and 'made up' – as in 'made an image of'

60

Word or phrase	This suggests
'Half sunk'	It's been there a long time and the sand has built up around it?
'shatter'd'	
'frown/And wrinkled lip'	
'sneer of cold command'	
'lifeless'	

2 Read line 8 again. Its meaning isn't immediately clear. Go back and re-read from the beginning of the sentence in line 3: 'Near them on the sand'. Think about whose **hand** and whose **heart** are being referred to. Here are some students' thoughts:

I think the poet suggests that the ruler 'mock'd' his people whose hands fed him ... he was just a parasite.

The sculptor 'mock'd' up the image of Ozymandias, and put his heart into his work, which is why it survives.

The statue is lifeless but the sculptor has carved the face so that the ruler's emotions and power survive.

3 What are your own interpretations and why?

4 Look closely at the final six lines.

- What aspect of the ruler Ozymandias is described in lines 9, 10 and 11?
- How do lines 12, 13 and 14 provide a contrast to this?

5 Shelley leaves the reader to work out the significance of the contrast between the words written on the pedestal and the description in the last three lines. Read this student's annotated version, which draws out some of the techniques Shelley uses to create this contrast:

Look on my works, ye Mighty, and despair!'
↙ — This is ironic, as there is **nothing** left!

Nothing beside remains. Round the decay
↖ — Contrast with previous line. Short, powerful sentence

Of that colossal wreck, boundless and bare,
The lone and level sands stretch far and away. ⟵
↖— Alliteration – repeated sounds, and ideas, that emphasise the huge, empty wasteland. Just endless desert

Long vowels to emphasise distance ⟶

6 Write a paragraph in which you explain how Shelley uses these poetic techniques to create a vivid contrast.

7 Now write another paragraph exploring your interpretations of what the description of the broken statue of a once-great ruler in an empty desert might imply about Shelley's view of power and powerful people.

Tasks

The poem explores the theme of power and what happens to the powerful. Select one of these tasks, and write a detailed analysis of the poem, referring in detail to words, phrases and poetic techniques that add to the meaning and impact.

1 Show how Shelley creates a negative picture of a powerful ruler, by referring closely to language and poetic techniques.

2 Choose **one** of the following statements and write two or three paragraphs explaining how the poem 'Ozymandias' illustrates and explores this idea:
- You can't outlive time.
- The greater you are, the further the fall.
- Everything ends in destruction and decay.
- Art is more powerful than rulers and kingdoms

Key features

- 'Ozymandias' is a sonnet, written in iambic pentameter, but with an unusual rhyme scheme compared to other English sonnets
- Vivid descriptive language which provides a contrast between an object and its surroundings

Key theme

- Contrasting the inevitable decline of all leaders and of the empires they build with their boastfulness and desire to achieve lasting greatness

COMPARE WITH
- 'Tissue'
- 'My Last Duchess'

'mind-forged manacles I hear:'

'London' by William Blake

'London' was written in 1794, as part of a collection of poems entitled *Songs of Innocence and Experience*. William Blake lived in London at the time of the Industrial Revolution when the city was expanding, and also at a time of political unrest. Wealth and poverty existed side by side.

⇨ First impressions

1. Read the poem at least twice. What view of life in one of the world's major cities at the end of the eighteenth century does it present?

2. Select three images from the poem that stand out for you as shocking or negative. For each, write a couple of sentences to explain what the image suggests to you, and any questions it raises for you about the poem. Here is an example of one student's ideas:

'every infant's cry of fear' – this is a shocking image as the poet suggests that all of the babies are crying out of fear. Early childhood should be a happy time. I wonder what they are so afraid of?

William Blake

⇨ Look a little closer

① Each verse is like a snapshot, setting out what the poet sees and hears as he walks through the streets of London. For each verse, note what the poet/traveller sees and hears. Choose a quotation from each verse to illustrate your commentary. Verse 1 has been done for you.

Verse	Sees	Hears	Quotation
1	People's faces showing signs of sickness and sadness	–	'Marks of weakness, marks of woe.'
2			
3			
4			

② Now look more closely at Verses 2 and 3. For each there are annotations and questions below. Read each verse carefully and give answers to the questions asked.

> ### ℛ KEY VOCAB
>
> **chartered** – a deed giving someone the right to own land, etc.
>
> **manacles** – handcuffs
>
> **harlot** – prostitute
>
> **blights with plagues the marriage hearse** – the reference to a harlot blighting the 'marriage hearse' with 'plague' is usually understood to refer to the spread of venereal disease, which is passed by a prostitute to a man and from him to his bride, so that marriage can become a sentence of death

---

Verse 2:

In every cry of every man,
In every infant's cry of fear,

⟵ Why does the poet repeat 'every' so many times?

In every voice, in every ban, ⟵

This probably means the rules and restrictions placed on people

The mind-forged manacles I hear:

⟵ How can a 'manacle' be forged in the mind? What is he getting at?

Verse 3:

How the chimney-sweeper's cry

⟵ Probably a child sweep. Why might the church find this appalling?

Every black'ning church appalls,

⟵ What does this image suggest? Is it linked to industrialisation in some way?

And the hapless soldier's sigh ⟵

Why might the soldier 'sigh'?

Runs in blood down palace walls.

⟵ Why might Blake pick out the church and the palace in this verse?

⇨ Exploring the detail

'London' offers an image of a city that is full of people who are suffering, living in poverty, where disease and violence are visible, and where the institutions of the state are powerless and may even be responsible for this state of affairs.

Part of exploring the poem in more depth is to understand how it builds up such a powerful picture of a city in just 16 short lines.

(1) On a copy of the poem, highlight, in different colours:
- images of suffering
- images of restriction of freedom, and imprisonment.

Write a sentence in which you summarise what the poem seems to be saying about life in London at this time.

(2) Find examples of:
- repetition of words and phrases
- the use of a regular rhythm to emphasise the images of suffering and violence.

Explain how these poetic devices add to the poem's effect on the reader.

(3) Look closely at how Verse 4 concludes the view of London. Take each line in turn, and use the question to develop your sense of what the writer is aiming to say:
- Line 1. What does the image 'midnight streets' suggest to you?
- Line 2. Why might Blake emphasise that the harlot is 'youthful'?
- Line 3. What is the effect of the infant being described as 'new-born'?
- Line 4. Look at the explanation of this line in the key vocabulary box opposite. What makes the line so powerful, and also so shocking? Give particular attention to the two words which conclude the poem.

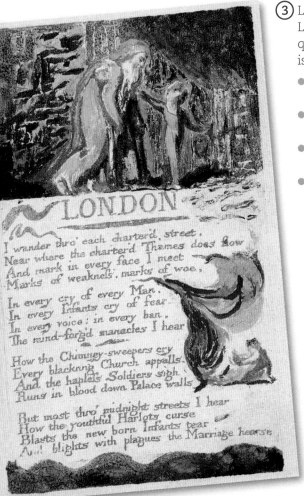

Tasks

1. Show, by making detailed reference to the poem and to the writer's use of poetic devices, how Blake creates a sense of London as a nightmarish place.
2. Choose one of the following statements about the poem, and write a response in which you justify your choice:
   - The ballad form is used to add to the effect of people's lives that are tightly restricted and controlled.
   - Blake describes a city that is without any redeeming or positive features.
   - The poem's power comes from the use of repeated images that emphasise everything that is wrong with life in an industrial city.
   - The poem 'London' was probably written to shock people into doing something about the society they lived in.
3. Jean-Jacques Rousseau declared in *The Social Contract* in 1762: 'Man is born free, and everywhere he is in chains.' How does Blake present this idea in the poem 'London'?

Key features

- Ballad form, four verses, iambic pentameter with rhyming couplets – a traditional English verse form
- Powerful imagery designed to shock the reader
- Repetition of key words and phrases

Key themes

- Dangerous industrial conditions, child labour, prostitution and poverty
- Lack of freedom, and suffering

COMPARE WITH

- 'The Prelude: stealing the boat'

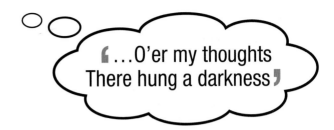

' …O'er my thoughts
There hung a darkness '

William Wordsworth

'The Prelude: stealing the boat' by William Wordsworth

'The Prelude or, Growth of a Poet's Mind' is an autobiographical poem by the English poet William Wordsworth. It was written in 13 long sections (or books) between the years 1798 and 1850. Wordsworth called it 'a poem on the growth of my own mind'. This extract is taken from a section based on Wordsworth's schooldays and boyhood in the Lake District.

⇨ First impressions

The extract starts like this:

> One summer evening (led by her) I found
> A little boat tied to a willow tree
> Within a rocky cove, its usual home.
> Straight I unloosed her chain, and …

(1) Without reading any further, note down your first impressions. What do you notice about the:
- style: think about the words – are they easy or difficult to follow and understand?
- location – what sort of place is being described?
- event – what is likely to happen?

⇨ Look a little closer

1. Read the whole extract. You will notice that it is a complete story, with a beginning, a development and a conclusion. It has five distinct sections.

2. On a copy of the extract, use this summary of each section to mark where each begins and ends:

   a) The boy 'borrows' a boat and sets off, on a beautiful evening, rowing across a lake.

   b) Enjoying his prowess as an oarsman, he decides to head further out down the lake.

   c) Suddenly he becomes afraid of something.

   d) He hurries back, rowing quickly, and returns home.

   e) Later he thinks about what he experienced and tries to make sense of it.

⇨ Exploring the detail

1. The extract is written to suggest that the storyteller (or narrator) is **telling us directly**. Find and mark on your copy of the poem different examples of this 'conversational' style. Look for:

   - conjunctions such as 'and', 'but' and 'when'
   - examples of the narrator telling us how he felt at certain key moments
   - vivid description of his actions.

2. A key theme in the poem is the contrast between two views of the natural world as:

   - a place of beauty and calm reflection
   - a place that exerts a powerful and sometimes frightening force, making the individual feel small and insignificant.

   Here are two examples of the poet's use of an image to suggest each perspective:

   ✳ *'Small circles glittering idly in the moon,'*

   ✳ *'the grim shape/Towered up'*

   Find three more examples of images that suggest natural beauty, and three that convey nature as a powerful, frightening force. Annotate your copy of the poem with your summary of what each image suggests to you.

3. Wordsworth uses **personification** to create the sense that the mountain peak, and other features of the natural world, seem to his mind to be alive, e.g. 'She was an elfin pinnace'.

Locate these four examples in the extract where the mountains are described using personification:

✱ *'nor without the voice/Of mountain-echoes did my boat move on;'*

✱ *'a huge peak, black and huge, …/Upreared its head.'*

✱ *'the grim shape/Towered up between me and the stars,'*

✱ *'like a living thing,/Strode after me.'*

For each, comment on the effect created for the reader.

(4) Re-read the final section of the extract, where the poet thinks back to his experience on the lake (from: 'but after I had seen/That spectacle,' to 'a trouble to my dreams').

What might it have been about his experience on the lake that so troubled the young Wordsworth?

Key features

- Written in blank verse
- Tells a complete story in a conversational style of a childhood adventure that turns out to have particular significance
- Use of images of the natural world to express contrasting perspectives, e.g. beauty versus dangerous and powerful forces

Tasks

1 Show how the poem takes us on a journey from the ordinary to the extraordinary.

2 'This is a poem about a child's realisation that the natural world is much more powerful and frightening than he realised.' Show how the language and use of imagery in this extract supports this view.

COMPARE WITH

- 'London'
- 'Storm on the Island'

Key themes

- The power of the natural world
- How an ordinary event can come to contain a sense of the extraordinary

'and I choose Never to stoop.'

'My Last Duchess' by Robert Browning

This poem is an example of a particular style of poetry called a **dramatic monologue**. The poem is set in Italy and, rather like a play, is based on three 'characters': Duke Alfonso II of Ferrara (who ruled from 1559 to 1597); his previous wife, the Duchess Lucrezia de Medici, who died aged 16 in 1561; and an emissary from the Count of Tyrol. Browning wrote the poem in 1842.

⇨ First impressions

1. Think about the phrase 'dramatic monologue'. What do the two words suggest to you?

2. Now analyse the title. It gives us a strong hint about what to expect from the poem:
   - If someone refers to another person as '**my** …' what might this suggest about the relationship, and how the other person is regarded?
   - If someone talks about 'my **last** …' what does this suggest?

3. Read the poem once. Record your immediate impressions:
   - Who is the speaker in the poem?
   - What impression do you gain of the speaker's character?
   - Towards the end of the poem we discover some information about the silent listener. What do we learn?
   - What seems to be the situation that the poem is based on?

⇨ Look a little closer

1. The first line sounds like the reply to a question. Write a new first line, which shows what the question was.

2. On a copy of the poem, write a series of detailed **stage directions**, setting out where the scene takes place, who is in it, and describing their actions, starting with:

The Duke pulls back a curtain to reveal …

🗨 KEY VOCAB

Frà Pandolf and Claus of Innsbruck – fictional painter and sculptor

mantle – a loose sleeveless cloak or gown

munificence – great generosity

pretence – claim

(3) In a dramatic monologue:

- the poem must have a speaker and a silent listener
- the reader often recognises that there is a **gap** between what that speaker says and what he or she actually reveals.

Focus on what the poem reveals about the Duke.

Find evidence in the poem of aspects of the Duke's character that are **implied** – i.e. not stated directly, but which we can work out as a reader from both what he says and how he says it. Record your ideas and impressions as shown below:

The Duke's actual words	What this reveals
'I call/That a piece of wonder,'	The Duke is proud of the painting
'I said/"Frà Pandolf" by design,'	He is 'name dropping' and hoping to impress his listener
'none puts by/The curtain I have drawn for you, but I'	
'She had/A heart – how shall I say? – too soon made glad,/Too easily impressed;'	
'her looks went everywhere.'	
'she ranked/My gift of a nine-hundred-years-old name/With anybody's gift.'	
'I choose/Never to stoop.'	
'his fair daughter's self, … is my object.'	

(4) Re-read the last section of the poem, from: 'Will't please you rise?'

Look back at your impressions. Re-read the poem. Write one sentence in which you summarise what kind of person the Duke reveals himself to be. Are you sympathetic towards him or not? Do you see some aspects of his character that are not very attractive?

(5) Focus on what the poem reveals about what the Duke thinks of the Duchess.

- What aspects of the Duchess's character, actions and attitude annoyed and angered the Duke?
- Find evidence that suggests that the Duchess stood up for herself, and wasn't 'submissive'.
- Find evidence of **one thing** above all that made the Duchess fall out of the Duke's favour.

⇨ Exploring the detail

① The Duke only hints at what happened to the last Duchess. Re-read the section of the poem from: 'Who'd stoop to blame/This sort of trifling?' to 'Then all smiles stopped together.'

Here are three possible explanations. Which do you think is most likely, based on the evidence from the poem?

- The Duchess decided she could take no more and left the Duke.
- The Duchess was banished – perhaps sent away to live in a convent as a nun.
- The Duchess was murdered by the Duke.

Write a short report in which you set out what you think may have happened, making reference to the poem to support your views.

② On a copy of the poem, add directions to an actor playing the Duke, and speaking the poem out loud.

- Select **five key lines** that reveal most about the Duke's character, and explain how they should be read.
- Identify and highlight **three sections** where the **use of punctuation** mirrors the twists and turns of speech. Show how the words should be said. For example:

> She had
> A heart – how shall I say? – too soon made glad,
> Too easily impressed; ↖
>
> *The Duke pauses, not because he can't think what to say, but for effect. He then delivers his big criticism. Sounds scornful*

③ On your copy of the poem, highlight every example of the use of the personal and possessive pronouns 'I', 'me' and 'my'. You should find over 20 that the Duke uses to refer to himself. What does this add to the impression you have formed of his character?

④ Do the same for the pronouns the Duke uses to refer to the Duchess. What does this add to the impression you have formed of how the Duke treated the Duchess?

Tasks

1 In 'My Last Duchess', the Duke comments on a painting of his previous wife. Show how Browning uses a dramatic monologue to reveal far more than the Duke actually says about his character, his relationship with the Duchess, and what happened to her.

2 'This is a poem about the power that men, especially powerful men, can have over women.'
From your reading of 'My Last Duchess', how far do you agree with this view? Write a detailed essay in which you offer your ideas on what the poem has to say about the nature of power.

Key features

- Written as a dramatic monologue, in regular iambic pentameters
- Uses punctuation to mirror the features of speech
- Hides an important revelation until towards the end of the poem
- Reveals more about the main character than is actually said in the poem

COMPARE WITH

- 'Remains'

Key theme

- Power relationships in marriage

'Some one had blunder'd'

'The Charge of the Light Brigade' by Alfred, Lord Tennyson

The Crimean War (1853–56) was fought between Russia and an alliance of British, French and Turkish troops. On 25 October 1854, the British commander Lord Raglan ordered a group of 670 horsemen (the 'Light Brigade'), armed with only lances and sabres, to attack a Russian artillery battery during the battle of Balaclava. Of the 670 who set off, only 195 returned. Historians have suggested that the brigade was given the wrong order, and sent into a narrow valley where they were fired on from both sides.

Alfred, Lord Tennyson was Poet Laureate at the time, and published this poem six weeks after the battle. The poem is a dramatic narrative poem that re-creates the scene of the battle, and provides a strongly expressed view by the poet on the significance of the event.

⇨ First impressions

① Read the first verse two or three times.

a) What do you immediately notice about the way the poem is written?

Think about:

- how the poem uses rhyme
- the rhythm of the words
- repeated words and phrases.

b) Before reading on, make two predictions:

- Is the poem going to praise or criticise those who gave the orders to charge?
- Is it going to praise or criticise the soldiers who made the charge?

② Now read the rest of the poem. Were your predictions correct or not? Find two lines from the poem that indicate that the poet thinks that the:

a) soldiers should be praised for what they did
b) order to charge was a mistake.

⇨ Look a little closer

① Read the poem aloud. The use of a repeated rhyme scheme and the rhythm of the words are strong features of the poem. They convey the horsemen galloping forwards; the firepower they faced from the Russian guns (cannons); the actual fighting and the retreat and return of those who survived. Practise saying the words so that the action described is brought to life.

② Listen to an archive recording of Tennyson reading the poem aloud. This is from one of the first wax cylinder recordings ever made:

www.poetryarchive.org/poem/charge-light-brigade

③ Copy and complete the table below by summarising what aspect of the charge is described in each verse. Verse 1 has been done for you:

Verse	What is described?
1	670 horsemen are given orders to charge into 'the Valley of Death'
2	
3	
4	
5	
6	

④ What do you notice is different about Verses 2 and 6?

🗨 KEY VOCAB

Light Brigade – horsemen armed only with swords so that they can travel fast. Usually used to attack retreating troops

league – a distance of about three miles

blunder'd – made a mistake or miscalculation

battery – a place where one or more guns are located

volley – guns or cannons firing all at once

⇨ Exploring the detail

① Explore the way that the poem presents the actions of the Light Brigade. Find words and phrases from the poem that suggest that:

- the soldiers were brave and fought well
- the soldiers were faced by fierce opposition
- the brave soldiers were let down by those in command
- soldiers should never question an order
- the soldiers knew that they faced almost certain death.

② A key feature of the poem is the use of repeated words and phrases and sounds.

a) Find examples:
- that convey the relentless charge of the light horsemen; what else might this suggest about the charge?
- that convey the suicidal nature of the charge because of the strength of the opposing forces
- of alliteration in Verse 3 to emphasise the enemy fire
- of alliteration in Verse 4 to emphasise the damage inflicted on the Russian troops.

b) Verses 3 and 5 are very closely related, with lots of repeated lines. However, there are some important differences. Look closely at what has changed. On a copy of the poem, highlight the changes. Write a paragraph explaining what aspect of the charge is presented in Verse 5.

③ The line 'All the world wonder'd:' is repeated in Verses 4 and 6. Explore the two different meanings of 'wonder'd' in each verse. Write two sentences comparing the two meanings. For example:

In Verse 4, the world wonders ... whereas in Verse 6 ...

④ Read Verse 6 again.

There are four types of sentence in this short last verse. Find:
- a rhetorical question
- an exclamation
- a statement
- a command.

Explain how these different sentences convey what the poet wants to say, finally, about what happened.

Alfred, Lord Tennyson

⑤ Investigate the word 'honour', which is used right at the end of the poem. Re-read Verse 6 carefully. For which of the following reasons do you think Tennyson believes that the soldiers should be 'honoured'?

- Because they obeyed orders.
- Because they fought bravely.
- Because they were prepared to ride into almost certain death without questioning why.

Write a short explanation, using quotations from the poem to support your conclusion.

Tasks

You should use your knowledge and understanding of the poem to provide a detailed written answer, and use quotations from the poem to provide evidence for your views.

1 'The Charge of the Light Brigade' has been called 'a moving tribute to courage and heroism in the face of devastating defeat'.
   a) Present your detailed interpretation of the poem, showing how far you agree or disagree with this view.
   b) Include a paragraph where you discuss your reading of and response to the poem now, compared to that of a reader in 1860.
2 Show, by close reference to the poem, how the poet's use of poetic techniques creates an effective sense of direct, immediate action.

Key features

- Repetitive rhyme scheme
- Strong use of rhythm to convey action
- Emphasis on how the event should be understood and commemorated

COMPARE WITH
- 'Bayonet Charge'

Key theme

- Views of heroism, bravery and miscalculation in war

'Exposure' by Wilfred Owen

(But nothing happens.)

➡️ First impressions

Before reading the poem, think about the title: 'Exposure'. The noun **exposure** is linked to the verb **to expose**. It has several meanings.

① Study the images on this page and page 80. Which of these definitions of 'exposure' do you think are likely to be the ones that the poem is based on?

Now read this information about the poem:

'Exposure' was written by Wilfred Owen in 1917. It is based on his experiences as a soldier on the front line in the trenches in the First World War. The winter of 1917 was a particularly bitter, freezing one.

② Now read the whole poem. First, read through to get a general sense of what the poem **describes**. Then read it again, this time very slowly, and think about the **sound** of the words. Use the key vocabulary box on the opposite page to help with words that you may not know. Read it a third time, aloud. Experience the sound of the words as you say them.

③ Think back to the title. The poem describes night, dawn and early morning in the trenches.

- Who is 'exposed'?
- What are they exposed to?

> ### KEY TERM
>
> **Expose**
> - To leave unprotected (especially from the weather)
> - To be subjected to danger
> - To put on display for all to see
> - To let light into a film
> - To suffer and eventually die from the cold

KEY VOCAB

salient – what is known and understood as the most important piece of information; also, an outward bulge in a line of military attack or defence

gunnery – the operation of large military guns

glozed – a old word that combines 'gloss', 'glow' and 'glaze' to create a sense of shining

⇨ Look a little closer

(1) The poem is made up of eight verses. Read Verses 1–5 again and copy and complete the table below with your thoughts and ideas about each verse. Look closely at the poem to find evidence for what you decide. Verse 1 has been done for you.

	What do the soldiers feel, see and hear?	Words or phrases that convey the soldiers' experiences
Verse 1	Intense cold Silence and whispering Flares Confusion Fear	'the merciless iced east winds that knive us' 'Worried by silence, sentries whisper,' 'Low, drooping flares' 'confuse our memory of the salient' 'Worried … nervous'
Verse 2		
Verse 3		
Verse 4		
Verse 5		

(2) When you have completed the table, write two or three sentences in which you **summarise** the aspects of warfare that the poem conveys.

(3) Now read Verse 6 again, where the soldiers dream that they return home, but as 'ghosts'. Discuss these questions:
- Why are the fires only 'glimpsed'?
- What does the repetition of 'doors all closed: on us the doors are closed,' suggest about the soldiers' thoughts about returning home?

(4) Read Verse 7 again. Instead of describing an aspect of the experience in the trenches, it seems to provide the soldiers' answer to the earlier question: 'What are we doing here?' The soldiers wonder what they are dying for. What is their explanation?

(5) Read the **final verse**. It looks ahead to the future – the night to come and the return of the intense cold. Look closely at these words and phrases.

✳ 'frost will fasten' ✳ 'shaking grasp'

✳ 'Shrivelling … puckering … crisp' ✳ 'All their eyes are ice,'

For each, explain what the frost will do to the men.

(6) Look at the short last line in each verse.
- 'But nothing happens' occurs four times, including as the last line of the whole poem. What is the effect of this repetition?
- Look at the last lines in Verses 2, 5, 6 and 7. What do you notice about how these lines link to each other?

HINT

Think about 'kind fires'; 'suns smile true' …

79

⇨ Exploring the detail

1. Annotate a copy of the poem, using different colour pens to highlight examples of the following techniques that help to convey the sense of fear, boredom, misery and uncertainty felt by the soldiers:

   - Descriptions of the weather and natural elements including verbs, e.g. 'rain soaks, and clouds sag'.
   - Sounds of words – use of alliteration, e.g. the repeated consonant /s/ in: 'merciless iced east winds' and assonance, e.g. the long /o/ sound in 'Slowly our ghosts drag home'.
   - Use of personification – non-human elements are given human characteristics, e.g. 'Pale flakes with fingering stealth come feeling'.

   For each example that you highlight, write a short comment explaining the **effect** of the poet's choice of words. For example, a student wrote:

   By using the line: 'Pale flakes with fingering stealth come feeling for our faces' the poet conveys the sense that the snow is alive, and behaving like some kind of monster, or ghost even ('pale' and 'stealth' suggest something vaguely horrible, creeping up on you). This also suggests that the soldiers are frozen, perhaps with fear as well as cold, and can't resist.

2. The structure and form of the poem help to convey both meaning and impact. It is written in a series of eight five-line stanzas, using a rhyming technique called **half-rhyme** or **pararhyme**. Here is an example from Verse 2:

   - ... wire
   - ... brambles
   - ... rumbles
   - ... war

   Select another verse and identify the half rhymes.

   One student developed an interesting interpretation of the effect of the use of half-rhyme, linking it to the way the poem creates a sense of uneasiness:

The poem 'Exposure' is a commentary on the waste and pity of war. Like the war which 'is not as it should be', Owen's rhymes are not true either. The incompleteness of the half rhyme creates an uneasy feeling, things don't sound or feel right. This mirrors how the soldiers are feeling: uneasy and on edge; unsure and incomplete.

Tasks

1 This is a challenging and complex poem about the experience of soldiers in the trenches during the First World War. Discuss the following different interpretations, each of which is valid. Which do you **most** agree with, now that you have studied the poem in detail?

a) The poem is about how the soldiers just want to die and escape the war.

b) The poem suggests even God has turned His back on the soldiers.

c) The soldiers are shown to be suffering passively – there is no action and all they can do is wait for death.

d) The poem suggests the soldiers accept their duty and that they are being sacrificed for a just cause.

For your chosen interpretation, write a paragraph in which you justify your view, by making detailed reference to the poem.

Read this example of one student's ideas linked to statement d).

The poem 'Exposure' shows how the soldiers suffer because 'nothing happens'. There is a sense that the 'real hell' of the situation lies in the waiting (as seen in the repetition of 'But nothing happens'). However, by contrast, in Verse 5 the narrator describes an imagined, idealised rural scene. The dreamlike quality of this passage ('So we drowse, sun-dozed') and his question, 'Is it that we are dying?' suggests death as a desirable relief from their present torture.

2 Show how the main ideas about war in the poem are presented through the way that Owen uses language. Draw on how your understanding and appreciation of the poem has developed. Make reference to the ideas and experiences that the poem describes, and **analyse** the main techniques used, showing how they are effective.

Key features

- Creating strong images through personification; and the sound of words, using assonance and alliteration
- Use of the present tense
- Pararhyme or half-rhyme
- Repetition of key words and phrases

COMPARE WITH

- 'Bayonet Charge'
- 'The Charge of the Light Brigade'

Key themes

- Combat seen through the eyes of a soldier
- Suffering and isolation
- How extreme conditions can create a sense of helplessness and detachment from reality

> **❛Strange, it is a huge nothing that we fear.❜**

'Storm on the Island' by Seamus Heaney

Seamus Heaney wrote poems that combine a feeling for rural life with his experience of growing up living under the shadow of conflict in Northern Ireland. 'Storm on the Island' is an example of this.

⇨ First impressions

Reading this poem aloud will help you to understand one of its most important features – its tone of voice.

① Read through the poem silently.

② Now read the poem aloud. Think about the way it is written.

- What tone of voice seemed best suited to the poem? Angry? Sad? Conversational? Confident? Uncertain?
- Compare your ideas with others.

③ Find evidence in the poem that the 'speaker' is in conversation with somebody – possibly the poet.

④ The poem describes an islander's thoughts on living in an exposed place. Read the poem again, and, using a table like the one below, make a list of features of the island that we are either told about directly, or can infer.

Feature of the island	Evidence from the poem
Houses are built close to the ground	'we build our houses squat,'

KEY VOCAB

pummel – to hit repeatedly, usually with a fist

strafe – to bombard with shells or bullets

salvo – a number of bullets or bombs released at the same time

⇨ Look a little closer

Investigate the way the poem expresses the attitude of the islanders to where they live and the weather that they experience.

① Look closely at the opening two lines. Which of these words best describes the attitude of the speaker?

- Worried and anxious
- Confident
- Determined

② The speaker goes on to comment on the absence of vegetation – for example, there are no fields of hay, nor any trees. This suggests that the island is barren and very exposed. Look closely at these lines. What attitude does the speaker have to this?

③ Re-read the section that describes the action of the sea. How would you describe the attitude expressed here?

④ Look closely at the final four lines. Write two sentences summarising the speaker's attitude overall to the extreme storms that the island experiences.

⇨ Exploring the detail

Explore how 'Storm on the Island' uses language and some poetic devices to create the sense of how the storms affect those who live there, and how they deal with it.

① On a copy of the poem:

- highlight all of the words and phrases that use **military** terms to describe the storm, e.g. 'Exploding'; Heaney builds up a sense of the storm as a threat by creating the idea that the storm is like an aerial bombardment
- highlight all the pronouns: 'we', 'us'. What does the repeated use of these words suggest about the islanders?

② The speaker uses the word 'company' twice. Find and re-read these sections. Something about life on the island is being hinted at here. What might this be?

③ A feature of this poem is the way that the poet uses words with a common pattern of sounds, to add to what is being described.

Investigate these two examples:

> 'we build our houses squat,
> Sink walls in rock and roof them with good slate.'

④ Each of the words highlighted in Question 3 is **monosyllabic**. Explain how this choice of words adds to the sense that the houses are well built, strong and secure.

⑤

> 'the flung spray hits
> The very windows, spits like a tame cat
> Turned savage. We sit tight while wind dives
> And strafes invisibly.'

The repeated vowel sound 'i' (assonance) adds to the sense of the wind and spray whipping at the windows. This is also an example of **personification**. Find other examples of personification in the poem and write a paragraph in which you show how this poetic device adds to the effect of the poem.

⑥ Look carefully at the **form** of poem. It is 19 lines long, written in blank verse. It uses, mostly, the present tense.

- How does the use of the present tense add to the impact of the poem, and contribute to one of its themes – the power of nature?
- In an essay, one student wrote:

The poem is built like one of the houses: squat, firmly put together, with no loose bricks.

Find evidence to support this idea.

Tasks

You should use your knowledge and understanding of the poem to provide a detailed written answer, and use quotations from the poem to provide evidence for your views.

1 Show how Seamus Heaney conveys the power of nature, and the response of those who have to live with it, in 'Storm on the Island'.
2 'Strange, it is a huge nothing that we fear'.
  Show how the writer of 'Storm on the Island' manages to create a sense of a 'huge nothing' by the use of choice of vocabulary and poetic devices.

Key features

- Poem written in blank verse in a tightly controlled form
- Sound patterns of alliteration and assonance used to convey meaning
- Personification and imagery of warfare used to describe the effect of natural events
- Conversational style and tone of voice, using everyday language and the patterns of speech

COMPARE WITH

- 'The Prelude: stealing the boat'

Key themes

- The power of nature
- How people are able to remain strong and 'weather' many kinds of storm

> **‘** King, honour, human dignity, etcetera
> Dropped like luxuries **’**

‘Bayonet Charge’ by Ted Hughes

Written in 1957, this poem looks back to the experience of a soldier ordered to ‘go over the top’ from the trenches in the First World War.

⇨ First impressions

One way to think of this poem is as an account of a soldier’s waking nightmare. It might depict a true event, or it might convey a terrible dream rather than reality.

① Read it through to yourself once.

② Now read it again out loud. Try to get a sense of the rhythm of the lines and the way the pace changes in each verse.

   a) Try to communicate the sense of sudden action in Verse 1.

   b) What do you notice about the pace of the poem in Verse 2?

   c) Identify where the action resumes in Verse 2.

   d) Read Verse 3 in a breathless way to convey the panic and terror that the soldier experiences.

Think of this as a drama performance. Don’t worry here about understanding the full sense of every line, but convey in your reading:

- fear and panic
- bewilderment and a sense of ‘what am I doing here?’
- rising terror towards the end.

⇨ Look a little closer

On a copy of the poem, annotate your thoughts and ideas, using the following questions and prompts as a guide:

① Verse 1:
- What is the effect of starting with the adverb 'Suddenly'?
- Find and highlight all of the present participles (e.g. 'running'). What is the cumulative effect of this choice of words?
- How does line 3 **enact** the sense of 'stumbling' through mud?

② Verse 2:
- How does the rhythm of the lines 'slow down'? What happens to the way the sentences are structured to create a sense of time standing still?
- Find an example of 'enjambment' that conveys the sense that the soldier has 'almost stopped' in his forward charge.
- Work out what it is about his actions that 'bewilders' the soldier. What can't he fully understand?

③ Verse 3:
a) What, exactly, seems to happen in the last verse:
- to the hare?
- to the soldier's ideals and senses of patriotism?

b) How do you interpret the last two lines?

⇨ Exploring the detail

The poem is more than just a description and re-creation of a single event. It also expresses some thoughts about the nature of warfare, and what it does to those engaged in it.

① Find examples of imagery that show a rural setting destroyed by the brutality of war. For each example, explain how the image works, and the effect that is created for the reader, using a table like the one below.

Image	Explanation	Effect
'a green hedge/That dazzled with rifle fire'	Instead of 'dazzling' with sunlight, for example, the hedge is sparkling with bullets	Dreamlike image: bullets almost beautiful?

② Each verse contains lines that express the soldier's ideas about war. These are important to the poem and need to be thought about carefully. For each of the following, explain in detail what the poem is suggesting, or implying:

✸ 'The patriotic tear that had brimmed in his eye
   Sweating like molten iron from the centre of his chest, –'

✸ 'In what cold clockwork of the stars and the nations
   Was he the hand pointing that second?'

✸ 'King, honour, human dignity, etcetera
   Dropped like luxuries'

Tasks

Use your knowledge and understanding of the poem to provide a detailed written response, in at least three paragraphs, and use quotations from the poem to provide evidence for your views.

1 Show how the poem 'Bayonet Charge' conveys the way in which a soldier changes from a man with a sense of why he is fighting to someone who is just an instrument of war.

2 Write a detailed analysis of the poem 'Bayonet Charge' that shows how the way that the poem is written creates a sense of a nightmarish experience. Focus particularly on the use of rhythm and imagery.

Key features

- Three verses, using varied rhythmic effects to convey the action and the thoughts of the soldier
- Single event is captured, but given wider significance
- Vivid use of imagery to convey ideas of the mechanical destructiveness of modern warfare

Key themes

- Patriotism
- The brutality of war, and what war does to those engaged in it

COMPARE WITH

- 'Exposure'
- 'Kamikaze'
- 'The Charge of the Light Brigade'

‛ he's here in my head
when I close my eyes, ’

‘Remains’ by Simon Armitage

This poem is from a collection of poems *The Not Dead* (2008), based on interviews conducted with servicemen returned from active duty in a number of conflicts. This poem is based on an interview with a soldier who had fought in Iraq and concerns an event that happened while he was on patrol in Basra.

⇨ First impressions

1. Before reading the poem, write down two or three possible meanings of the word used as the title: ‘Remains’.
2. Read the poem, once, slowly, concentrating on making sense of the event that is recounted.

   - Who is speaking and telling the story?
   - Look back at your list of meanings of ‘remains’. How many of these might be relevant to the poem? You may need to add a further definition now that you have read the poem.

3) The poem is an account of a moment of violence and its aftermath. Select two or three images from the poem that immediately stand out for you as shocking because of the way they describe the violence. Give your first impressions using a table like the one below. One example has been completed for you.

Line or image	My impression
'I see every round as it rips through his life'	'rips' shows how the bullets tear through his body; 'life' shows how his whole life is gone in an instant

⇨ Look a little closer

The poem is set out in eight verses (seven four-line verses, and a final two-line verse).

1) The first four verses could be subtitled: 'What happened'.

   a) Re-read the final four verses. Verse 5 starts: 'End of story, except not really.'

   b) Write your own subtitle for the second half of the poem that captures the essence of this section.

2) Look more closely at what the narrator of the poem reveals about his view about the events, through what he says and the way he says it. Copy and complete the table by finding quotations from the poem that support each of the following statements.

Statement	Quotation
They were only obeying orders	
The narrator is immediately affected by the suffering they cause	
One of the soldiers acts in an unfeeling way	
The narrator re-lives what happened	
He can't erase the memories	
He feels responsible, perhaps guilty	

⇨ Exploring the detail

① Explore the nature of the speaking voice in the poem. On a copy of the poem, highlight words or phrases that are:

- typical of informal, casual, everyday language
- written in the continuous present tense (e.g. 'all three of us open fire')
- repeated.

For each, make a note that explains the effect of these language choices. What do they add to your impression of the persona (the soldier) who is telling the story?

② Some parts of the poem convey the reactions and feelings of the soldier in 'heightened' metaphorical language.

a) For each of the following examples, write a sentence that explains how you respond to what the words suggest, and explain how the use of a metaphor adds to the effect:

> 'blood-shadow'
> 'I blink/and he bursts again through'
> 'the drink and the drugs won't flush him out –'
> 'dug in behind enemy lines,'
> 'some distant, sun-stunned, sand-smothered land'
> 'near to the knuckle,'

b) Think carefully about the final line of the poem:

> 'his bloody life in my bloody hands'

c) Practise saying this line:

- in a casual, off-the cuff way – where 'bloody' is just a swear word
- emphasising the literal meaning of 'bloody' – to convey a sense of the horror of the memory.

What do you notice about where you place emphasis and stress in the second way of saying this?

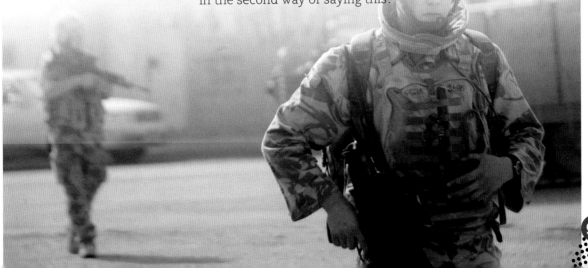

1 'We know this is poetry and not a documentary or transcript of an interview.'
Write a detailed commentary and analysis of the poem that shows how it contains a blend of poetic rhythm and imagery, and colloquial speech. Explain how both of these aspects combine in the poem and what they convey about the impact of war on a soldier after the event.

2 About 'Remains' Simon Armitage wrote: 'The poem … revolves around a key "flashback" scene, requiring the soldier to re-visit the very incident he was desperately hoping to forget.' Show how the poem powerfully conveys this sense of the **trauma** of an event that can't be forgotten.

Key features

- Formal structure of four-line verses, some using iambic pentameter, with a final two-line verse
- A blend of poetic rhythms and imagery with the language and tone of colloquial speech
- A flashback memory, re-lived as if it were still unfolding, using the present tense

Key theme

- The effect of warfare on the thoughts and feelings of a soldier after the event

COMPARE WITH

- 'War Photographer'
- 'Bayonet Charge'

On reaching the top of the hill I traced the inscriptions on the war memorial

'Poppies' by Jane Weir

The poem 'Poppies' was written in 2009 by Jane Weir in response to a request from the poet Carol Ann Duffy to ten poets to each write a poem in response to present-day wars and conflicts.

The poem isn't a straightforward account of war. Instead it tackles the subject of war by presenting a personal view in a very specific situation. It is also a poem that lends itself to interpretation. When asked what the poem is 'about', Jane Weir replied: 'I think it's important to let the reader have space to make up their own mind.'

⇨ First impressions

(1) Read the poem once. Now read it again, slowly, allowing yourself to think about the experience that is being related.

(2) On a copy of the poem, note down your immediate thoughts and ideas about the following questions:

a) Who is the speaking voice – the 'I' in the poem?
b) Who is the 'you' that is referred to many times?
c) What **might** be the experience that is being described here:
- A mother grieving for a son killed in a war?
- A mother sending her young son off to school for the first time?
- A mother fearing for the future of her son in a world full of conflict?
- Add any ideas of your own.

(3) Highlight or underline any lines or phrases that seem to need further careful thought so that you can understand and appreciate the poem more fully.

⇨ Look a little closer

① 'Poppies' is a poem that tells a story – it relates a series of linked events.

- Highlight all of the references to time – the words and phrases that move the story forwards in a chronological way. For example, the opening words are 'Three days before'.
- Revisit your first thoughts about the experience that the poem relates – and add to or amend your initial ideas. In particular, look at the questions you asked on your initial reading, and the sections that you wanted to look at in more detail.

② The 'voice' in the poem is that of a mother, describing how she feels, and acts, as she says goodbye to her son. Search through the poem to find words and phrases that:

- show how she feels **protective** and **loving**
- indicate that she is **anxious** or **fearful**
- suggest that the son is of school age
- suggest that she forces herself to hide her emotions.

Add these to your annotation of the poem.

③ Look closely at the last verse. The narrator does three things. For each, develop your **interpretation** of what each action suggests about her feelings about war:

- ✳ *'traced/the inscriptions on the war memorial,'*
- ✳ *'leaned against it like a wishbone.'*
- ✳ *'I listened, hoping to hear'*

⇨ Exploring the detail

① Explore how the form of the poem contributes to its effect. It is written in four verses in a fairly regular pattern (6 lines, 11 lines, 12 lines, 6 lines). However, if you look carefully you will see how the writer has deliberately started many sentences in the middle of a line, for example:

- ✳ *'of my face. I wanted to graze …'*
- ✳ *'you were little. I resisted the impulse'*

Find other examples. What might this suggest about the way the narrator feels?

② Add to your annotated copy of the poem by highlighting all of the possessive pronouns: 'your', 'my'. What effect does the repetition of these create?

③ The poem is set in a home. Highlight in one colour all of the **domestic and personal details**, e.g. 'white cat hairs'. In another colour, highlight all the words and phrases that are related to **war**, **injury** and **conflict**.

What is the effect of these contrasting images and details?

⬤ KEY VOCAB

Armistice Sunday (or 'Remembrance Day') – commemorated every year on 11 November to remember the members of armed forces who have died in the line of duty

blockade – surrounding a place, by armed forces, to prevent anyone leaving

intoxicated – drunk, or exhilarated, highly excited

④ The poem contains a number of images and references to:

- poppies
- needlework and embroidery
- caged birds and doves

Find these and add to your annotations.

Why do you think the writer included these details? How do they add to the way that the poem explores a particular reaction to the idea of warfare and conflict?

Task

'Poppies' is about both one mother's feelings on a particular day, and the feelings of all mothers about war'.

1 This is one student's view of the poem. What are your thoughts on the poem? Write a detailed commentary on the poem, exploring different interpretations, justifying your ideas by making close reference to, and analysing key words, phrases and lines.

Key features

- The poem tells a personal story
- Powerful use of imagery
- Use of symbolism
- Use of the caesura to interrupt a line of thought

COMPARE WITH

- 'Kamikaze'

Key theme

- A personal view of war from a mother's perspective

spools of suffering set out in ordered rows.

'War Photographer' by Carol Ann Duffy

This poem provides a set of images or snapshots of a war photographer carrying out an aspect of his work and gradually allows us to appreciate his thoughts and feelings about what he does.

⇨ First impressions

Before reading the poem:

1. Look carefully at the image above and the one on page 97, and think about the job of a war photographer. Select two or three words from the following list which seem to you to best describe the job that a war photographer does:

   exciting   dangerous   intrusive   necessary   important
   unhelpful   brave   foolhardy   exploitative

   Discuss: What might be the hardest feature of being a war photographer?

2. These are some lines from the poem. Choose two as captions to go with each of the photographs above.
   * ✱ 'He has a job to do.'
   * ✱ 'running children in a nightmare heat.'
   * ✱ 'A hundred agonies in black-and-white'
   * ✱ 'to do what someone must'

3. Now read the poem twice. On the second reading, read slowly, and think about what is being described.

96

④ Discuss and decide which of the following statements best sums up your first response to the poem (you can choose more than one):

- The photographer hates his work.
- Once safe at home, the photographer is reminded of terrible things he has witnessed.
- The photographer believes he is doing an important job.
- The photographer knows that his photographs will be ignored by the public.
- The photographer feels guilty about taking photographs of suffering and bloodshed.
- The photographer has to stay calm and dispassionate in order to be able to do what he does.

For each statement you have chosen, find some key words, phrases or lines from the poem that support your ideas.

⇨ Look a little closer

① The poem is written in a very regular way, in four verses, each with six lines using a regular rhyme scheme. Each verse is like a single snapshot, which gradually reveals a bit more about the way the photographer feels about the work he does.

Take each verse in turn; read it carefully, and then, for each, describe and explain what the verse reveals about what is going through the photographer's mind. Support your ideas with references and quotations to the poem.

Here is how one student started her answer to this task:

Verse 1: Alone in his darkroom, the photographer starts to develop his latest batch of photographs. The line 'spools of suffering' suggests that he knows that he has taken lots of photos of awful things, but they are in 'ordered rows' which implies that he is very careful in the way he goes about his job ...

KEY VOCAB

spool – a reel for winding photographic film

intone a mass – say or recite the words of a mass in a Catholic church

'All flesh is grass' – a line from the Bible, suggesting that human life is fragile, easily cut down

➡ Exploring the detail

Work through these questions, which will help you to gain a fuller understanding of the poem and an appreciation of how the poet, Carol Ann Duffy, uses structure, words and images to make the poem work.

(1) Think about the word 'finally' in the first line: 'he is finally alone'. What does it suggest about the photographer's life and work?

(2) Find a description in the last verse that connects directly to the idea of 'spools of suffering'.

(3) Find examples of religious imagery in Verse 1. What might this suggest about the way the photographer feels about the photos he takes?

(4) What do the lines: 'his hands which did not tremble then/though seem to now' suggest?

(5) Why might the pain be 'ordinary' when he thinks of home?

(6) What is the effect of describing one of the photographic images as 'a half-formed ghost'?

(7) We are told that: 'The reader's eyeballs prick/with tears between the bath and pre-lunch beers'. What does this suggest about:

- the impact that the photographs have on viewers back in the UK?
- the contrast between where the photographs were taken and the photographer's home country?

(8) The last verse explores the connections between the war zones, the photographs, and how they are used. Look carefully at the way the poem moves from the images, to the editor, to the publication, to the reader, and then back to the photographer. Read the last two lines of the poem very carefully. The poem deliberately leaves the reader to interpret these lines. What is your interpretation of where the photographer is flying to, and who are 'they' in the line: 'they do not care'?

Offer your interpretation, starting with these words:

In the final two lines of the poem, the war photographer is flying above ...

Tasks

1 Read these extracts, which are taken from an article in which a national newspaper picture editor reflects on the difficulty of choosing which war photographs to include for publication:

'Over the years, I have seen many disturbing photographs … Sometimes I wonder why a photographer hasn't turned away from a scene, but their place is to record; ours is to edit.'

'… in the end, what right do I have as a picture editor to censor what people can see?'

2 Write a short piece in which you explain what the poem reveals about the conflicts and concerns that go through the mind of a war photographer.

3 Show how the poem uses imagery to present the contrast between the things the photographer experiences in his work, and when he is on home soil.

4 Write a short explanation of how the **structure** of the poem contributes to what the writer wants to convey about the work of a war photographer.

Key features

- Four six-line verses with a rhyming couplet at the end
- Religious imagery
- Contrasts between a peaceful homeland and war-torn locations

Key information

Belfast – the capital city of Northern Ireland, site of a prolonged and bloody conflict between the British Army and a terrorist campaign waged by the Irish Republican Army (IRA) between 1971 and 1997

Beirut – the capital city of the Lebanon, where there was violent civil war in the late 1970s, and war with Israel in 1986 and again in 2006

Phnom Penh – the capital city of Cambodia in Southeast Asia, where in 1975 a group called the Khmer Rouge took control and imprisoned, tortured and executed between 1 and 2 million citizens

COMPARE WITH

- 'Remains'

Key theme

- The horrors of war versus an indifferent public

" this
is what could alter things "

Imitiaz Dharker

'Tissue' by Imtiaz Dharker

Imtiaz Dharker was born in Pakistan, and moved to Glasgow, Scotland, when she was one year old. She now divides her time between Wales, London and Mumbai. She has often described herself as feeling 'stateless'. As well as being a highly respected poet, she is a documentary film maker and accomplished artist. The poem 'Tissue' explores themes of culture, identity, and the permanence of structures.

⇨ First impressions

① Before reading the poem, pause to think about the title. Make a short list of meanings and connotations of the word 'tissue'. Try to think of as many as you can.

② Read the poem twice, the second time as slowly as you can, allowing the words to sink in.

③ Using the list that you wrote in answer to Question 1, and what you gain from your first readings of the poem, list all the ways in which the meaning of 'tissue' is explored.

⇨ Look a little closer

① Focus more closely on what aspects of the idea of 'tissue' the poem explores in some of the verses. Copy and complete the following table:

Verses	What aspect of 'tissue' is explored?	Key quotation
1–3	Very thin, see-through paper, containing family names, dates and history	'Paper thinned by age or touching,'
6		
9		

(2) Look at Verses 4 and 5. Here the poet asks a couple of 'what if?' questions.

- For each verse, explain what is suggested.
- What might the poet be suggesting by wondering about 'borderlines' becoming transparent, or 'shifting'?

(3) Now consider Verses 7–9. Re-read them carefully. Explain what the poem is suggesting that an 'architect' could do with 'all this'.

(4) Start to explore some possible themes in the poem – ideas that the poem seems to be interested in. On a copy of the poem, highlight lines, phrases and words that suggest:

- lives beginning, being lived and ending
- structures, countries, borders and features of the landscape.

(5) Use two different colour highlighters to mark sections of the poem that refer to:

- solidity and certainty
- change and impermanence.

(6) Write a paragraph in which you describe how the poem establishes and develops contrasting sets of ideas and images.

⇨ Exploring the detail

(1) Focus on the following lines from the poem, and offer your thoughts on the questions posed:

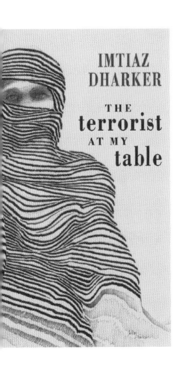

An architect could use all this,

What is being referred to here?

Who might the 'architect' be?

...

find a way to trace a grand design

A 'design' for what?

with living tissue, raise a structure
never meant to last,

Look ahead to the last line of the poem

...

turned into your skin.

What kind of 'transformation' is suggested here?

IMTIAZ
DHARKER

THE
terrorist
AT MY
table

(2) A feature of this poem is the way it suggest possibilities, rather than certainties. It does this partly through the use of 'modal' verbs such as 'could' and 'might'.

- Find the lines where this occurs and highlight the verbs.
- For each instance, explain what is being suggested, or thought possible or desirable.

(3) The poem contains some important images that link to the themes and ideas that it explores. For each of the following, explain what the image or collection of images suggests:

* *'Paper that lets light/shine through,'*
* *'The sun shines through/their borderlines,'*
* *'let the daylight break/through capitals and monoliths,'*
* *'fly our lives like paper kites.'*

(4) Verse 1 refers to 'what could alter things'.

Use your growing understanding of the poem to suggest some possible interpretations of what the poet is suggesting could be 'altered' and why.

Tasks

1 Show how the poem explores the various meanings of the word 'tissue'.
2 Write a detailed commentary on the poem 'Tissue' showing how it uses **contrast** to explore ideas about how a person's identity is formed, and what is important in life.
3 'The poem "Tissue" builds layer upon layer'.
Show how this description of the poem applies both to the ideas and themes in the poem, and to the way the poem is constructed.

Key features

- Carefully structured in nine four-line verses, with a single final line
- Contrasting ideas and images of permanence and impermanence
- Modal verbs to express uncertainty and possibility

Key theme

- How lives are lived and are changed by the structures that surround us

COMPARE WITH

- 'Ozymandias'

❝I have no passport, there's no way back at all❞

'The Emigrée' by Carol Rumens

Carol Rumens is a British poet. She has travelled extensively in Eastern Europe and Russia, and often uses this experience in her poems. This poem was first published in the collection *Thinking of Skins: New and Selected Poems* (1993).

⇨ First impressions

1. Read the poem twice, the second time slowly. Note down any words or phrases that are repeated. What do you notice about these?

2. An émigrée is a person who has been forced to leave a country for political or social reasons. Search through the poem and highlight words or phrases that are connected to the idea of being **forced to leave somewhere**.

3. What do the opening words: 'There once was a country' suggest about what to expect from the poem?

⇨ Look a little closer

1. For each verse, write a short commentary that sums up what aspects of 'emigration' are explored. For example, one student wrote the following about Verse 1:

The poet says she left a country as a child, but has a really clear memory of it. It's a happy memory, as shown by the image of it as a 'bright, filled paperweight.'

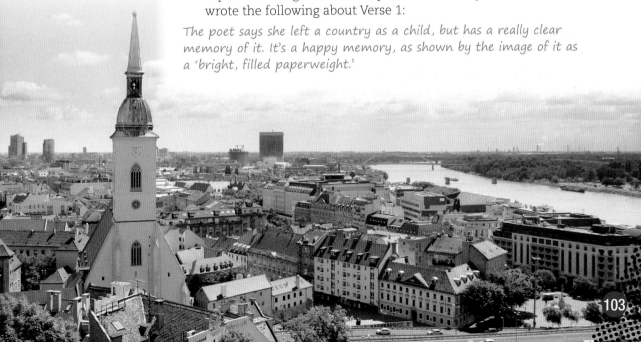

(2) What do we learn about the poem's narrator? Make a set of notes in two columns as follows:

What we know	What is hinted at
Left home country as a child	The country may no longer be as it is remembered

(3) Identify and highlight on a copy of the poem two sets of contrasting images and ideas in the poem that are related to:
- light – especially sunlight
- restriction, lack of freedom and oppression.

Explain what the use of this contrast suggests to you about the ideas that the poem explores.

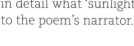 Exploring the detail

(1) The poem takes the literal meaning of 'émigrée' and explores how it can also be used to represent other kinds of isolation or forced absence. This is called an **extended metaphor**.

Re-read the poem, and as you do, think about what other kinds absence might be implied.

Comment on the effects created by the following:
* ✷ 'time rolls its tanks'
* ✷ 'frontiers rise between us,'
* ✷ 'I have no passport,'
* ✷ 'My city takes me dancing through the city of walls.'

(2) Look at the last four lines of the poem.

Explain how the poet uses images relating to terror and interrogation to express positive ideas about memory and identity.

(3) Return to the way that the image of sunlight is used in the poem. Write a paragraph in which you explore in detail what 'sunlight' might represent to the poem's narrator.

Tasks

1 One student wrote: '"The Emigrée" is about different kinds of "emigration" – including being separated from a lover'. What are your thoughts on the poem? Write a detailed commentary on the poem. Write one paragraph for each verse, and a fourth concluding paragraph, exploring different interpretations. Strengthen your choice by making close reference to, and analysing key words, phrases and lines.

2 Show how the poem 'The Emigrée' uses specific language and imagery to explore different ideas about oppression and banishment.

Key features

- Formal structure: three eight-line verses
- Imagery relating to light, contrasted with images of darkness and oppression
- The idea of being an émigrée as an extended metaphor to explore other interpretations of the word, and the concept of 'having to leave' a place or person

COMPARE WITH

- 'Tissue'
- 'Checking Out Me History'

Key themes

- How an émigrée holds onto memories
- Ideas of freedom and banishment
- The power of state oppression
- Enforced departures

‘And sometimes, she said, he must have wondered which had been the better way to die.’

‘Kamikaze’ by Beatrice Garland

A Japanese woman explains to her children what happened to their grandfather in the war.

⇨ First impressions

Before reading the poem:

(1) Look at the images on this page and page 108. They show a Japanese plane having crashed deliberately into a US warship in 1944, and Japanese kamikaze pilots preparing to fly suicide missions.

(2) Read the definition of ‘kamikaze’ in the key vocabulary box opposite.

(3) Now read the first verse of the poem.

(4) What thoughts and emotions might a kamikaze pilot have experienced just before setting off on a suicide mission?

(5) Now read the rest of the poem. What do we learn about the father’s suicide mission? Note down quickly, from your first reading of the poem, some possible reasons why he might have turned back for home.

kamikaze – During the Second World War, Japanese airmen were sent on suicide missions, crashing planes filled with bombs into Allied naval vessels in the Pacific Ocean. Nearly 4,000 pilots were killed as a result. A belief in the importance of death instead of defeat, capture and shame was a key element in Japanese military culture. For a Japanese military man, the Bushido code of loyalty and honour until death was one of the main traditions

'a flask of water, a samurai sword' – ceremonies were carried out before kamikaze pilots departed on their final mission. The kamikaze shared ceremonial cups of sake (rice wine) or water known as *mizu no sakazuki*. Many kamikaze pilots took their swords with them, if they were officers

Incantation – a magic formula, spell or chant

⇨ Look a little closer

'Kamikaze' explores a daughter's thoughts as she tries to explain to her children why their grandfather did not complete his mission as a suicide pilot.

1. Read the poem again twice.

2. Search through the poem and highlight images that suggest **life**, **colour**, **beauty** and **energy**. For example, in Verse 3 the shoals of fish are described as 'flashing silver'.

3. The narrator hints and suggests, but doesn't explain fully why her father turned back. Read Verses 2–5 again. Look carefully at the way the poem describes what the daughter thinks her father 'must have' seen and thought. Use this information to explain what the poem suggests as reasons for why he turned for home rather than carrying out his mission.

⇨ Exploring the detail

1. Look closely at how the poem is structured.
   - How many sentences are there?
   - In what ways is each sentence different?

2. For each sentence, in a copy of the table below, sum up the content and the main idea about war that is explored or expressed.

Sentence	Content and ideas
1	
2	
3	

3. What is the impact of the final short sentence?

4. Look carefully at the language in Verses 2–5 again. The poem contrasts two very different things: the pilot setting out on a suicide mission to destroy an enemy ship; and how what he sees below him prompts some childhood memories. Write a short explanation for each of the following images, suggesting how they add to the sense of the father choosing life and safety over certain death:

   ✳ 'fishing boats/strung out like bunting'
   ✳ 'like a huge flag waved first one way/then the other'
   ✳ 'brothers waiting on the shore'
   ✳ 'bringing their father's boat safe'
   ✳ 'awash/with cloud-marked mackerel,'

5 Re-read the section in italics in Verses 6 and 7.

- The poem doesn't explain why his wife and neighbours treated the father in the way they did after his return. Why might they have behaved like this?

6 Comment on the final two lines. What is being suggested about the choice the father made? Refer back to the rest of the poem in your answer.

Tasks

1 Show, by making close reference to the poem, how 'Kamikaze' explores the idea of a military man choosing life over death, and the consequences of his choice.

2 Show how the poem 'Kamikaze' presents us with different viewpoints on the pilot's decision to return home safely, rather than continue with his mission. In your response, make reference to the viewpoint of the:
- father
- daughter
- wife and neighbour
- children.

Key features

- Formal structure of seven verses, each of six lines
- Vivid imagery to contrast with the destructive nature of war
- Unusual use of sentence lengths

Key theme

- Attitudes to warfare: honour and shame

COMPARE WITH

- 'Poppies'
- 'Bayonet Charge'

> ❝Bandage up me eye with me own history
> Blind me to me own identity❞

'Checking Out Me History' by John Agard

John Agard is a black British poet, originally from Guyana, in the Caribbean. At school in Guyana, he was taught a version of British history. In this poem he explores the relationship between history, identity and language.

Read the poem several times to gain a fuller appreciation of its meaning, impact and the ideas that lie 'behind' the poem. Use the following questions and prompts to help you to develop a detailed annotated copy of the poem.

⇨ First impressions

① Look at the **shape** of the poem. This will give you a sense of its overall structure. Notice how the lines are set out in 'blocks' – not exactly verses in the traditional sense. Notice also the three sections written in italics.

② Start your annotations by thinking about the title and the opening three lines:

- How does the writer create an immediate sense of difference through his use of language?
- Who might he be referring to as 'Dem'?
- What is the effect of the opening repetition of 'Dem tell me'?

John Agard

(3) Write a comment on the next two lines. What does the use of 'Bandage' and 'Blind' suggest the writer thinks about the kind of history he has been taught?

⇨ Look a little closer

(1) Read the rest of the poem.

(2) Now listen to a recording of John Agard performing the poem: www.poetryarchive.org/poem/checking-out-me-history

(3) Annotate the poem to show lines, and sections, where the poet's speaking voice changes to convey:

- annoyance
- amusement and humour
- outrage
- confidence and certainty
- reverence or respect.

(4) 'Dem' is repeated 17 times through the poem. The poet is offended by being prevented from knowing about his own history. Now that you have read the poem several times, and listened to the poet reading it, write down as many possible explanations of who 'Dem' might be.

(5) Find all the references to figures from 'white' history. Many are not genuine 'historical' references. Why might the poet have decided to include these figures from nursery rhymes and folk tales?

(6) At the start of the poem, the poet is subjected to being 'told', and uses the powerful image of his eyes being 'blinded' to his own history and identity. It is an image of suffering and oppression. Look at the final four closing lines. What do you notice about the change of tone, especially the use of the verbs 'checking' and 'carving'?

⇨ Exploring the detail

(1) On your annotated copy of the poem, find and highlight every reference to 'light' and 'sight'. Where do these mainly occur?

(2) Compare the rhythm of the 'Tell me' sections with the different rhythm in the italicised sections (the parts of the poem where figures from black history are described). If the rhythm of the 'tell me' sections is repetitive and hammers home the point being made, how would you describe the italicised sections?

(3) Now, using the ideas and insights you have gained from Questions 1 and 2 above, write a paragraph in which you explain how the poem moves back and forth between contrasting sections, and the effect that this creates for the reader.

KEY VOCAB

Toussaint L'Ouverture – a former slave who rose to become leader of the revolution in Haiti in the late eighteenth century

Nanny de Maroon – a leader of freed slaves in Jamaica in the first part of the eighteenth century who set up their own community and successfully resisted British rule

Shaka – powerful and respected king of the Zulu nation (1787–1828)

Caribs and Arawaks – the original inhabitants of an area of South America and the Caribbean islands

Mary Seacole (1805–81) – born in Jamaica, she lead a varied life, which included providing food, lodging and support for servicemen in the Crimean War. In 2004 she was voted the greatest black Briton.

Tasks

You should use your knowledge and understanding of the poem to provide a detailed written answer, and use quotations from the poem to provide evidence for your views.

1 Read these words, which were written in a newspaper article by Paul Reid.

'If my teacher had told my class that the black presence in Britain could be measured in millennia, and that we were not just … tagged onto the end of the colonial story I might have had a different sense of belonging; I might have had a different idea of what was possible; I might have seen something to aspire to.'

Show how, in 'Checking Out Me History', John Agard explores the same theme.

2 '"Checking Out Me History" is a playful approach to a serious topic.' How far would you agree with this view?

3 Show how John Agard creates a distinctive 'voice' in the poem, and also how this voice varies, and why.

Key features

- Use of a non-standard English Caribbean dialect
- Contrasts of tone, imagery, rhythm
- A direct speaking voice that makes the poem dramatic and best appreciated when read aloud

COMPARE WITH
- 'Tissue'
- 'The Emigrée'

Key theme

- The relationship between history, culture and identity

Writing a comparison answer

Here are two examples of a comparison question in the GCSE examination:

Read each question carefully. What, exactly, are you being asked to do? Underline the key instruction words in each of these questions.

(1) Compare how attitudes to war are presented in 'Poppies' and one other poem from 'Power and Conflict'.

(2) Compare the ways that poets present views and ideas about power in 'Ozymandias' and one other poem from 'Power and Conflict'.

When you answer a comparison question you need to:

1 Compare two poems:
- One poem will be chosen for you and printed in the examination paper.
- Select a second poem to use for your comparison. It needs to be an appropriate one.
- Discuss the **similarities** and **differences** between the two poems.

2 Analyse and explain how, or the ways that an idea, an attitude or a theme is presented or expressed.

3 Show your understanding of the methods used in each poem:
- **structure** – its form and how this contributes to its meaning and effect
- **word choices** and **poetic techniques** to convey effects and add to the meaning
- **tone**, or **attitude** – the way that the poem shows how the poet (or perhaps a character or speaking voice in the poem) thinks and feels.

4 Express your personal view and interpretation of what each poem is saying or implying about the theme or ideas.

How to write a good answer to a comparison question

① Prepare your answer

Use and adapt a planning grid like the one below so that you can decide what to include in your answer.

Focus of the question: e.g. 'how attitudes to war are presented'	
Poem 1	**Poem 2**
Similarities	
Ideas/theme Form and structure Word choices and poetic techniques Tone and attitude	Ideas/theme Form and structure Word choices and poetic techniques Tone and attitude
Differences	
Ideas/theme Form and structure Word choices and poetic techniques Tone and attitude	Ideas/theme Form and structure Word choices and poetic techniques Tone and attitude

② Plan your essay

Identify any key words in the essay question, and make sure that your answer focuses on exactly what the question asks you to do. Sort out what your main points are going to be and how you will organise your ideas using the following:

- A short opening paragraph: briefly explain which poems you will write about (titles and poets), and give an initial outline of the main points of comparison you intend to make. Show that you are setting out to write in a comparative way.
- At least three main paragraphs where you ensure that you write about both poems, cross-referencing ideas. Refer to the poems in detail, commenting, analysing and interpreting. Select some key quotations that you will use as examples.
- A conclusion where you provide your personal views or original ideas and sum up what you have concluded about the two poems.

You will need to learn how to prepare and plan an answer quickly, in examination conditions. To start with you will probably take a longer time than will be available in the examination, but this is a skill to improve through practice.

③ Stitch your ideas together

A good comparison essay is one which not only focuses on the question, but also has lots of good ideas that 'cohere' (fit together) so that your thinking is made clear to the reader. To do this, as you write, use a range of **cohesive devices** – words and phrases that link or connect your ideas up. Some of these will be within a paragraph, while others link across sentences or even paragraphs, for example:

> **Although** Poem X shows how ... in Poem Y the writer ...
>
> **In contrast** to ... or because of this ...

Cohesive words and phrases	
Add	also, furthermore, moreover, and, for example, especially
Contrast	however, nevertheless, on the other hand, but, instead, in contrast, yet, though, at least, in fact, by comparison
Concede	although, nevertheless
Reinforce	besides, anyway, after all
Explain	for example, in other words
Sequence	first, first of all, then, next, finally
Indicate cause and effect	and so, because, since, so, consequently, as a result, thanks to this, because of this, thus

④ Use appropriate terminology

As you have worked on the poems in this book, you have encountered, understood and used a wide range of useful terms to describe exactly what a writer has done to make a poem 'work' and have an effect on the reader. In a comparison essay, when you write about the **way** that a poet presents ideas, or the **methods** used to express a view, you should describe their techniques and methods by using the appropriate terminology.

Caution: only use a term if it is linked to a point you are making about the effect of the technique or approach. You get no marks for simply spotting techniques.

⑤ Provide an evaluative response

Don't just describe, explain or comment. Make sure that you also write about your **appreciation** of a poem's qualities, and your **interpretation** of what a poem seems to you to be striving to express.

Remember: most poems, especially good ones, can't be reduced to a summary; they don't communicate a single meaning. Poems are full of concentrated language; they often hint and suggest at ideas and feelings that aren't immediately obvious. Cecil Day-Lewis, who was Poet Laureate from 1968 to 1972, said this: 'We do not write in order to be understood; we write in order to understand.'

As a reader you bring your experience and ideas **to** a poem. A good comparison essay should show that you have thought about the poems, have **concentrated** your attention on them, and have developed your views, your interpretation. To achieve a higher level, you should show that you can see different possible interpretations, rather than settling for just one.

Tasks

1 For each of the two questions on page 112, practise the two initial stages – preparation and planning – before writing your essay using the formats provided.

2 Read this example of a student's opening paragraph for Question 1.

Question 1: Compare how attitudes to war are presented in 'Poppies' and one other poem from 'Power and Conflict'.

In Jane Weir's poem 'Poppies' the writer provides a mother's perspective on wars and conflict. The poem seems to be a very personal one. Although we don't know whether the events in the poem are autobiographical or the poet is imagining how the mother feels, the poem is written in a very personal way. In contrast, 'War Photographer' by Carol Ann Duffy gives us the voice of a male war photographer ('In his darkroom he is finally alone') who has returned from a conflict zone with a set of horrific photographs. In this poem we meet a person who has experienced war directly, whereas in 'Poppies', war is either in the past as the poet talks about 'Armistice Sunday' and the inscription on a War memorial, or is a vague fear for the future.

3 Annotate a copy of this paragraph to show:
- an outline of the main point of comparison between the two poems
- two examples of cohesive words and phrases that connect up ideas
- an example of a similarity
- an example of a difference.

4 Write your **opening paragraph** for Question 2. Focus on setting a **comparative tone**, explaining the poems you have chosen, and outlining the main ideas that you will explore in the rest of the essay.

5 For either Question 1 (using the opening paragraph above), or 2, now write the rest of your comparative essay.

6 **Selecting which poems to use in comparison**

Copy and complete the table on page 116. You can either work on this as you work with the poems, or after you have completed this work, as a way of revising and summarising. Use categories from this list – and add your own:
- how power declines
- combat seen through the eyes of a soldier
- patriotism, duty and honour
- the brutality of war, and the effect of war on combatants
- the relationship between power, culture and identity
- personal views of war and conflict
- how war and conflicts are presented in the media
- states and borders
- individual freedom
- freedom and oppression
- the power of the state
- the power of the natural world
- power relations in a marriage

Poem	Aspect(s) of the theme presented	Additional comments including method and form
'Ozymandias'		Sonnet
'London'	Individual freedom; the power of the state	
'The Prelude: stealing the boat'		Blank verse
'My Last Duchess'	Power relations in a marriage	Dramatic monologue
'The Charge of the Light Brigade'		
'Exposure'		
'Storm on the Island'		
'Bayonet Charge'		
'Remains'	The effect of war on combatants	
'Poppies'		
'War Photographer'	How war and conflicts are presented in the media	
'Tissue'	Freedom and oppression; states and borders	
'The Emigrée'		Extended metaphor
'Kamikaze'		
'Checking Out Me History'	The relationship between power, culture and identity	

The Unseens

Introduction

⇨ Thinking about poetry

This part of the book deals with Paper 2, Section C, Questions 1 and 2. Section C is the last part of Paper 2 and it asks you to write about two poems that you will probably not have seen before. You will be asked to analyse and comment on how two poets use language to achieve effects and meaning, using appropriate terminology.

You will be using the same skills that you used for the Section B part of the paper, although the questions will be worded slightly differently and the poems will probably be new to you.

In this part of the book you will practice the skills you have already learned:

- ⊕ understand and respond to poems
- ⊕ use a critical style and references to support your response
- ⊕ analyse the language, form and structure of poems
- ⊕ understand how poets create meaning and effects
- ⊕ compare poets' use of language, structure and form to achieve meaning and effects.

⇨ What will you be asked to do?

You need to answer **both** questions in Section C. You do not have to choose which questions to answer. Two poems will be printed on the examination paper.

Question 1 asks you to write about the first poem and is worth 24 marks. You should spend around 30 minutes on this question.

Question 1 will guide you to consider one aspect of the poem, so you cannot just write anything about it. You need to make sure your response is relevant to the question.

Question 2 asks you to compare the second poem with the first poem (the one that you wrote about for Question 1). This question is worth 8 marks. You should spend around 15 minutes on this question.

Question 2 will also give you guidance. It will ask you to write about similarities and differences between the ways the two poems are written.

When you answer this question, your comparison must focus on the **poet's methods only**. Again, you must make sure your response is appropriate and relevant to the question.

Section C is worth 32 marks altogether. Section A is worth 34 marks and Section B 30 marks so you can see it is worth your while to make sure you are well prepared for Section C of Paper 2.

⇨ The mark scheme: what does it mean?

Question 1	
Level 6 (21–24 marks)	The key word here is '**exploratory**'. A response at this level digs deeply into the text, examining and evaluating a writer's use of language, form and structure.
Level 5 (17–20 marks)	The key word here is '**thoughtful**'. A response at this level will be a more detailed consideration of both task and text. A candidate at this level may well offer alternative interpretations and use a more tentative style, considering a range of effects created by the writer's uses of language, form and structure.
Level 4 (13–16 marks)	The key word here is '**clear**'. A response at this level will be clearly focused on the task and text, using a range of effective, supporting details/quotations. The effects created by the writer's uses of language, form and structure will be fully explained.
Level 3 (9–12 marks)	The key word here is '**explained**'. A response at this level will have some focus on the task, using references to support points. Candidates at Level 3 will explain some of the reasons for their responses to the task and text. The effects of a writer's methods will be identified but perhaps not fully explained.
Level 2 (5–8 marks)	The key word here is '**supported**'. A response at this level is likely to have some focus on the task and will offer details/quotations to back up points made. A Level 2 response may well identify a method used by the writer, giving an example, but without actually identifying its effect upon the reader.
Level 1 (1–4 marks)	The key word here is '**simple**'. A response at this level may not be focused on the task and will probably not offer any supporting details or quotations. The response might refer to a writer's method ('the poet uses similes') but will not give an example of it.
Question 2	
Level 4 (7–8 marks)	The key word here is '**exploratory**'. A response at this level digs deeply into the two poems, comparing the writers' use of language, form and structure. Points will be analysed with judicious use of subject terminology. The effects of writers' methods will be convincingly examined in the comparison.
Level 3 (5–6 marks)	The key word here is '**thoughtful**'. A response at this level will be a more detailed consideration of both poems. A candidate at this level will offer a comparison, using subject terminology effectively, that considers a range of effects created by the writers' uses of language, form and structure. A Level 3 response will compare the effects of writers' methods on the reader.

Question 2 *(continued)*	
Level 2 (3–4 marks)	The key word here is 'relevant'. A response at this level will show a good understanding of the poets' methods and the comparison points will be relevant, with some use of subject terminology. Candidates at Level 2 will explain the reasons for their responses to the poems. The effects of the writers' methods will be compared but not fully explained.
Level 1 (1–2 marks)	The key word here is '**some**'. A response at this level is likely to make some links between the writers' use of language, structure and form and will offer some details/quotations to back up points made. A Level 1 response may well compare some of the writers' methods, but without actually identifying their effects upon the reader.

⇨ What you need to know about Section C

(1) **How many poems do I have to read?**

You have to read two poems.

(2) **How long should I spend reading and how long writing?**

Spend at least 5 minutes reading each poem. For Question 1, aim for 5–7 minutes reading and 20 minutes writing. For Question 2, spend 5 minutes reading and 10 minutes writing.

(3) **How many times should I read each poem?**

At least twice.

(4) **How long should I spend on Question 1?**

You should spend no more than 30 minutes on Question 1.

(5) **What if I run out of time?**

If you've planned your answer well you should still be able to finish your essay using note form. You won't get full credit, but you will get more marks than if you continue in long form but only get two-thirds of an answer written.

(6) **What if I don't understand one of the poems?**

There will always be something you understand about the poems. Remember to read each poem at least twice and slow down on the second read, really focusing on what the poet is trying to say and what the poem makes you think about. As you write, refer back to the poem and you will probably find more that you understand.

(7) **What if I can't think of anything to say about both poems?**

You will always be able to find something to say! Focus on what the poem makes you think about, and how it explores or expresses thoughts, ideas and feelings.

(8) **If the poems include words that I don't know, what should I do?**

If the words are very obscure, there will be a note telling you what they mean. Usually though, the poems will not have obscure words or terms. If you don't know a word, look at the context and have a guess. But don't obsess over it – it isn't always necessary to understand every single word to write a good response. Don't let it knock your confidence.

(9) **Suppose I don't like either of the poems. What should I write about?**

You don't have to like the poems to write about them. Just be sure to write about the two poems that are in front of you.

(10) **How much should I write for each answer?**

As a very rough guide, your Question 1 answer should be about 300 words and your Question 2 answer about 150 words but don't worry too much about length. Focus on writing what you want to write clearly, and managing your time wisely so that you finish your answers. A shorter, focused answer with evidence of deep, critical thinking will gain more marks than something which is long, rambling and does not answer the question or hit the level criteria.

Approach the unseen poetry questions with optimism. If you worry too much, you won't do yourself justice. The questions are not written to trick you; they simply ask you to engage with the ideas in the poems and show that you have thought carefully about the methods the poets use.

Effective reading techniques

This section deals with Question 1 of Section C. For this question you need to write about one poem, giving consideration to one particular aspect, which will be specified in the question.

In this section you will learn how to:

- get an initial overview of an unfamiliar poem
- read and re-read a poem slowly
- read a poem 'aloud in your head'
- look at the detail in a poem
- annotate a poem with a purpose in mind
- build your understanding of a poem.

To do well in this question you need to be able to get a quick overview of a poem and then re-read it in detail to build your understanding. You will be using the same skills that you used to read the poems in the Anthology.

1. Read the title and the whole poem once at your normal reading speed.

Try with this poem.

Poem 1: 'Impressions of a New Boy' by Marian Collihole

This school is huge – I hate it!
Please take me home.
Steep stairs cut in stone,
Peeling ceiling far too high,
The Head said 'Wait' so I wait alone,
Alone though Mum stands here, close by.
The voice is loud – I hate it!
Please take me home.

'Come. Sit. What is your name?'
Trembling lips. The words won't come.
The head says 'Speak', but my cheeks flame,
I hear him give a quiet sigh.
The room is full – I hate it
Please take me home.

A sea of faces stare at me.
My desk is much too small.
Its wooden ridge rubs my knee,
But the Head said 'Sit' so though I'm tall
I know that I must try.
The yard is full – I hate it.
Please take me home.

Bodies jostle me away,
Pressing me against the wall.
Then one boy says, 'Want to play?'
The boy says, 'Catch' and throws a ball
And playtime seems to fly.
This school is great – I love it.

(2) What is the poem generally about? Make a few notes on your initial thoughts.

(3) Read the poem again, this time more slowly. Linger over the words and phrases. Say some of them out loud (in the exam, you can read them 'aloud in your head'). This time, ask yourself: What are the main feelings expressed in the poem?

(4) Read the poem once again, paying attention to the detail. Make a note of any powerful words or poetic techniques (similes, metaphors, imagery) that the poet has used.

(5) Look at the rhythm and rhyme, and structure (verses, lines, punctuation) in the poem. Does anything strike you about the methods the poet has used?

(6) Annotate a copy of the poem by highlighting (with a highlighter pen or by underlining or circling) three words or phrases that surprise or interest you, or slightly puzzle you, or seem important to the poem.

As you highlight, make a comment or ask yourself a question about the part you have selected.

Here is one student's annotations for Verse 1 of the poem.

This school is huge – I hate it!
Please take me home.
Steep stairs cut in stone,

Do the words 'steep', 'cut' and 'stone' make the stairs seem unfriendly and cold?

Peeling ceiling far too high,

The school is uncared for – or is it just old?

The Head said 'Wait' so I wait alone,
Alone though Mum stands here, close by.
The voice is loud – I hate it!

Is the child a girl or a boy? How old is he or she? Maybe only five or six? Or older?

Please take me home.

(7) Add your ideas, and answer the questions/comments, if you can.

(8) Continue to highlight the poem, choosing sections that you particularly 'like' – this might be because of the sound of the words, or lines; or because you are struck by a particularly interesting image.

There may be parts of the poem that you don't particularly 'like'. If so, highlight these sections as well. Annotate the poem with your thoughts on why you have selected these.

This is how another student annotated Verse 1.

This school is huge – I hate it!
Please take me home.
Steep stairs cut in stone,

I think it is clever how the poet uses 'st', 'c' and 't' to emphasise the hardness of the stone steps

Peeling ceiling far too high,
The Head said 'Wait' so I wait alone,
Alone though Mum stands here, close by.

I like the way the repetition of 'alone' emphasises the child's sense of isolation – however, Mum is nearby so why does he or she feel lonely?

The voice is loud – I hate it!
Please take me home.

I like the way this repetition makes the reader feel sympathy for the child. Are the words spoken aloud? This makes me remember what it is like to start a new school when everything is strange and frightening

(9) Review the title. Add your thoughts as to why the poem is called this on your annotated version.

(10) Read the poem one last time. Notice how each time you read it, you build a deeper understanding of the poem. Ask yourself: What am I learning about the experience that the poet is describing here?

For example, you might notice:

- the simple language and rhythm that the poet uses, as if written (or spoken) by a child
- the way the last line of each verse disrupts the rhythm to emphasise the feeling
- the poet's use of short pieces of dialogue for variety
- how the poet gives us more information about the boy as the poem develops
- how the poet brings the poem full circle by repeating the first line in the last line, with two important word changes to show how the boy's feelings have changed.

(11) Now think again about the aspects of the poem that the Unseen question asks you to focus on. You should be ready to start planning your answers.

⇨ Exam practice 1

In the exam, you need to allow yourself 5–8 minutes to read the question and the poem before you start writing your answer. You should annotate the poem with your ideas as you read it – quickly the first time and then re-reading it more slowly at least once.

(1) Read this Paper 2 Section C exam Question 1:

In 'Impressions of a New Boy', how does the poet present the speaker's feelings about the school?

(2) What is the question specifically asking you to do?

(3) This is how a student started to annotate the poem in the exam, ready to write the answer to the question. Notice how the student's annotations are specifically focused on the question.

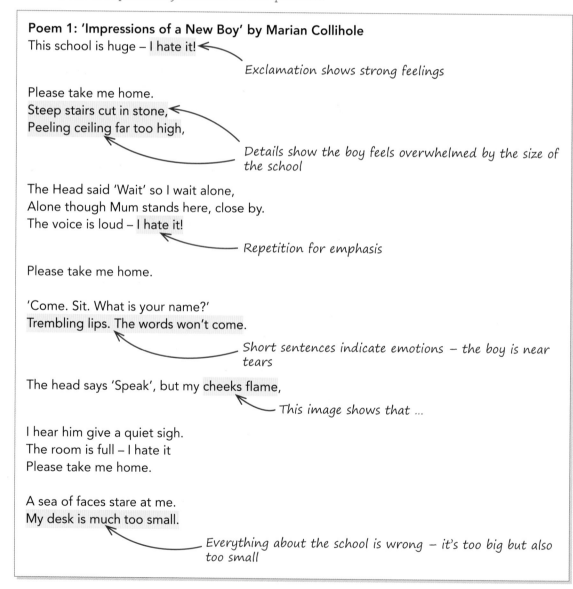

Poem 1: 'Impressions of a New Boy' by Marian Collihole

This school is huge – I hate it!

Exclamation shows strong feelings

Please take me home.
Steep stairs cut in stone,
Peeling ceiling far too high,

Details show the boy feels overwhelmed by the size of the school

The Head said 'Wait' so I wait alone,
Alone though Mum stands here, close by.
The voice is loud – I hate it!

Repetition for emphasis

Please take me home.

'Come. Sit. What is your name?'
Trembling lips. The words won't come.

Short sentences indicate emotions – the boy is near tears

The head says 'Speak', but my cheeks flame,

This image shows that ...

I hear him give a quiet sigh.
The room is full – I hate it
Please take me home.

A sea of faces stare at me.
My desk is much too small.

Everything about the school is wrong – it's too big but also too small

Its wooden ridge rubs my knee,
But the Head said 'Sit' so though I'm tall
I know that I must try.
The yard is full – I hate it.
Please take me home.

Bodies jostle me away,
Pressing me against the wall.
Then one boy says, 'Want to play?'

This word at the start of the line marks a turning point in the boy's feelings – from feeling out of place to feeling …

The boy says, 'Catch' and throws a ball
And playtime seems to fly.
This school is great – I love it.

④ Write your own answer to the exam question. You can use some of the annotations given above if you wish, or use your own notes and ideas if you prefer.

⇨ Exam practice 2

This is another sample Question 1 from Paper 2, Section C. Follow the steps you used with Poem 1.

① Read the exam question first, and then the poem.

In 'In Mrs Tilscher's Class', how does the poet present the speaker's feelings about school?

Poem 2: 'In Mrs Tilscher's Class' by Carol Ann Duffy
In Mrs Tilscher's class
You could travel up the Blue Nile
with your finger, tracing the route
while Mrs Tilscher chanted the scenery.
"Tana. Ethiopia. Khartoum. Aswan."
That for an hour,
then a skittle of milk
and the chalky Pyramids rubbed into dust.
A window opened with a long pole.
The laugh of a bell swung by a running child.

This was better than home. Enthralling books.
The classroom glowed like a sweetshop.
Sugar paper. Coloured shapes. Brady and Hindley
faded, like the faint, uneasy smudge of a mistake.
Mrs Tilscher loved you. Some mornings, you found
she'd left a gold star by your name.
The scent of a pencil slowly, carefully, shaved.
A xylophone's nonsense heard from another form.

Over the Easter term the inky tadpoles changed
from commas into exclamation marks. Three frogs
hopped in the playground, freed by a dunce
followed by a line of kids, jumping and croaking
away from the lunch queue. A rough boy
told you how you were born. You kicked him, but stared
at your parents, appalled, when you got back home.

That feverish July, the air tasted of electricity.
A tangible alarm made you always untidy, hot,
fractious under the heavy, sexy sky. You asked her
how you were born and Mrs Tilscher smiled
then turned away. Reports were handed out.
You ran through the gates, impatient to be grown
the sky split open into a thunderstorm.

② Now write your answer to the question. Write about 300 words.

Comparing poets' methods

Just as you did when you worked on comparing poems in the Anthology, you need to use your skills of comparison to answer Question 2 in Section C.

In the following pages you will deepen your understanding of comparison and practice how to:

- identify aspects of language, structure and form in both poems
- compare two poets' methods by analysing language, form and structure
- write a comparison of two poems.

However, the comparison you do for Question 2 is slightly different to the ones you did for the Anthology poems because:

- you will need to read and compare two poems that will probably be unfamiliar to you
- to do well in Question 2 you need to compare the way poets use language, form and structure to create effects in two poems. The question does *not* ask you to compare the content of the poems. You must focus on comparing the poets' **methods**.

When you compare the two poems, you need to focus on the similarities and differences in the methods the poets use and the effects they achieve whilst shaping your response to answering the examination question.

(1) Read the two poems from Section 1 on page 121–122 and 125–126 again.

(2) Remember that for this question you are focusing on methods and effects. Just as you did for the poem in Question 1, you need to annotate a copy of the Question 2 poem for comparison with the first. As before, ask yourself questions to help your comparison.

Why is annotating a poem helpful?

- It helps you to focus on certain words and phrases and search out deeper meanings of the words and images. This deepens your understanding of the poem.
- The examiner will expect you to be able to support (prove) your ideas and interpretations by close reference to the poem.
- If you have annotated important language features, words and phrases when you read a poem, you'll be able to find them quickly when you are writing your answer. Referring to them in your answer shows you have thought about the poem and points you make, and this will earn you higher marks.

TIP

The words 'both' and 'however' are useful for making comparisons.

TIP

A simple introduction to comparing two poets' methods is, 'Both poets use interesting methods – sometimes similar and sometimes different.'

③ Look at this student's annotations to compare Verses 1 and 2 of Poem 2 with Poem 1.

Poem 2: 'In Mrs Tilscher's Class' by Carol Ann Duffy

In Mrs Tilscher's class
You could travel up the Blue Nile

— Poet uses 'you' (not 'I' as in Poem 1). This makes the poem more inclusive, as if it is a shared memory or one that the reader will empathise with

with your finger, tracing the route

— No rhyme scheme – free verse, compared to Poem 1 which has a definite rhythm and a clear rhyme scheme. One effect of this is to make Poem 1 seem more restricted, like the boy at school, while Poem 2 is freer, as if the poet allows the speaker to freely associate her memories

while Mrs Tilscher chanted the scenery.
"Tana. Ethiopia. Khartoum. Aswan."
That for an hour,
then a skittle of milk
and the chalky Pyramids rubbed into dust.
A window opened with a long pole.

— This is the poet's own memory of school, filtered through the eyes of the adult. Details like the window and the milk and the bell show that it happened quite a long time ago

The laugh of a bell swung by a running child.

— The tone is optimistic and happy – happy memories of primary school. This is very different from Poem 1

This was better than home. Enthralling books.

— Use of past tense – Poem 1 is in the present tense. So, this speaker is older, looking back. The speaker in Poem 1 is a child. This gives a nostalgic tone to Poem 2 compared to Poem 1

— Completely opposite sentiment to Poem 1

The classroom glowed like a sweetshop.
Sugar paper. Coloured shapes. Brady and Hindley
faded, like the faint, uneasy smudge of a mistake.
Mrs Tilscher loved you. Some mornings, you found
she'd left a gold star by your name.
The scent of a pencil slowly, carefully, shaved.

Both poems use sensory descriptions – touch, sounds, sight, smell – but in Poem 2 the richness of these shows the child's enjoyment of school while in Poem 1 the effect is to make the reader feel school is an unwelcoming place

A xylophone's nonsense heard from another form.

(4) Continue the comparison by annotating Verses 3 and 4 of Poem 2.

(5) Comparison grids offer a very useful method of finding similarities and differences between poems. You have already used a comparison grid to compare poems in the Anthology.

Use your annotations to complete a comparison grid like the one below for Poems 1 and 2. The Question 2 to bear in mind when you make your comparison is:

In 'Impressions of a New Boy' and 'In Miss Tilscher's Class', the speakers describe their feelings about school. What are the similarities and differences between the ways the poets present those feelings?

Focus of the question: the ways the poets present their feelings about school			
Poem 1		Poem 2	
Similarities	What are the effects?	Similarities	What are the effects?
Form and structure		Form and structure	
Word choices and poetic techniques		Word choices and poetic techniques	
Tone and attitude		Tone and attitude	

Differences	What are the effects?	Differences	What are the effects?
Form and structure		Form and structure	
Word choices and poetic techniques		Word choices and poetic techniques	
Tone and attitude		Tone and attitude	

6. Read this part of a student's response to the question.

Both poems show the speakers' feelings about their experiences in primary school. However, in the first poem the speaker feels lonely and out of place: the school is 'huge' and the room is 'full' but the desk is 'much too small' – the new boy is struggling to feel at home in a strange place. This feeling is emphasised by the repeated line, 'Please take me home.' In contrast, the speaker in the second poem felt happy to be at school. She says, 'this was better than home'. This difference in feelings is further shown by the language the poets use. For example, in the first poem the poet uses hard images of steep stone stairs and a desk with a wooden ridge, and the boy is pressed and jostled in the playground, which shows he feels uncomfortable and out of place. By comparison, in the second poem the poet draws on rich sensory imagery of colours, light, sounds and smells ('the classroom glowed like a sweet shop' and 'the scent of a pencil, slowly, carefully shaved'). The poet's use of these images shows that the speaker has happy, loving memories of being in the classroom.

7. This response would be given a Level 2 in the exam. How would you improve it?

- Has the student covered methods and effects in both poems?
- Has the student found similarities *and* differences in methods and effects in the poems?
- Has the student made points about the writers' use of language, structure and form?
- Does the paragraph contain comment and analysis of the writers' methods?

Make improvements to the paragraph and then write the next paragraph.

⇨ Exam practice 3

① This is another sample Question 2 from Paper 2, Section C. Read the question first, then the poem. Follow the steps you used before to annotate the poem.

In 'Impressions of a New Boy' and 'I Am Very Bothered', the speakers describe their feelings about a school memory. What are the similarities and differences between the ways the poets present those feelings?

Poem 3: 'I Am Very Bothered' by Simon Armitage
I am very bothered when I think
of the bad things I have done in my life.
Not least that time in the chemistry lab
when I held a pair of scissors by the blades
and played the handles
in the naked lilac flame of the Bunsen burner;
then called your name, and handed them over.

O the unrivalled stench of branded skin
as you slipped your thumb and middle finger in,
then couldn't shake off the two burning rings. Marked,
the doctor said, for eternity.

Don't believe me, please, if I say
that was just my butterfingered way, at thirteen,
of asking you if you would marry me.

---

② A student has started to complete a comparison grid for this question. Complete the grid, adding your own thoughts from your annotations. Focus on the form and structure, word choices and poetic techniques, tone and attitude, and then the effects of each.

TIP

In the exam you are strongly advised to spend at least five minutes reading the second poem alongside the first poem before you start writing your answer.

Focus of the question: the ways or methods poets use to describe their feelings about a school memory			
Poem 1		**Poem 2**	
Similarities	What are the effects?	Similarities	What are the effects?
Form and structure Autobiographical, possibly based on a real memory	*Makes it personal and immediate for the reader*	Form and structure Autobiographical, possibly true memory	
Word choices and poetic techniques		Word choices and poetic techniques	
Tone and attitude Uses first person	*Use of 'I' makes the poem personal and vivid*	Tone and attitude	
Differences	What are the effects?	Differences	What are the effects?
Form and structure Some short sentences show speaker feels upset Direct speech	*We feel sympathy for the speaker*	Form and structure Long sentences carry the reader through Speaker addresses one person as 'you' Speaker is 'I' – very personal Very clinical and detailed description of what he did No clear rhythm – free verse	*We don't feel sympathy for the speaker*
Word choices and poetic techniques Use of repetition and patterned language		Word choices and poetic techniques Very plain and simple language – direct address to the reader	
Tone and attitude Innocent tone achieved through limited vocabulary, short sentences and simple syntax elicits reader's sympathy for the speaker, a child		Tone and attitude Humorous and mock-apologetic tone - the speaker says he is 'very bothered', but is he really apologising? His attitude is ambiguous Clearly an adult speaker	*Sarcastic tone creates a sense of distance between reader and speaker*

(3) Now write your answer to the question. Write about 150 words.

Approaching the exam

In this section you will learn how to plan your answers to Questions 1 and 2 in Section C. You will learn how to:

- structure your answers
- think as you write
- write to time
- check your answer.

For both questions, you must make sure your answer is relevant to the question you have been asked. Make sure you read the question carefully and bear it in mind as you read each poem.

So that you don't get confused, it is wise to tackle Question 1 first before you read the poem for Question 2. When you are planning your answer, make sure you include a short introduction. Remember to refer to the question to show that you are on task.

Identify three or four points that you can develop into paragraphs. Include details and quotations from the poem to support each point. Make sure you include a personal response and use appropriate subject terminology.

Remember a conclusion. You could end with a final idea about the key aspect that the question has asked you to address.

When you are planning your Question 2 answer, remember that a good comparison connects methods together so that you guide your reader through.

You can choose either of the following approaches.

⇨ Approach 1

- Write about the language, structure and form of Poem 1 first.
- Then write about the language, structure and form of Poem 2, referring back to Poem 1 and making comparisons.
- Add a final paragraph that sums up the similarities and differences with regard to the question.

⇨ Approach 2

- Compare your points for each poem in turn, bringing out similarities and differences.
- For example, Poet 1 uses repetition to show that the speaker feels nervous, while Poet 2 uses it to create a feeling of joyful exuberance. Both poets use simple, everyday language to create a sense of personal immediacy and credibility.
- Add a conclusion that sums up how you have answered the question, with reference to your points.

The second approach is trickier and requires more careful planning, but is more impressive if you can pull it off! It is probably the method that most examiners recommend.

Some useful phrases to use in your comparison

- Compared with …
- In comparison to …
- Both …
- However, …
- While in [poem] the writer … , in [poem] the writer …
- Whereas …
- Like/Unlike …
- Just as …
- In the same way …
- Consequently …
- Therefore …
- Similarly …
- In contrast, …
- On the other hand, …
- Also, …
- Again …

When you make a point, always try to support it with a quotation. Show that you understand what the quotation means and how the language contributes to the point you are making.

A useful way to structure your points is:

- give a main point about the poem (related to the question)
- support the point with a quotation
- explain how the language is used by the poet
- talk about the effects that the poet has created.

In the exam, you will need to do your planning quickly. Once you have four or five points in a logical order you can start writing. Keep thinking of and referring back to the poems as you write and if other ideas come to you, work them into your answer.

For Question 2, remember that you will already have ideas about the poem you've read for Question 1. Your focus now is to find points of comparison in the poets' methods and effects for *both* poems and create your plan in 3–5 minutes. You could use a simplified comparison grid like this one to plan your answer.

TIP

A top-level response will explore alternative interpretations ('It could mean this, but it could also be seen as this…').

Focus of the question:	
Poem 1	**Poem 2**
Similarities	
Form and structure	Form and structure
Language	Language
Effects	Effects
Differences	
Form and structure	Form and structure
Language	Language
Effects	Effects

Or you might find it easier to annotate each poem directly, having them side by side and marking sections of text 'S' for similarity and 'D' for difference. Experiment and find the method that works best for you.

Leave yourself a couple of minutes at the end so that when you have finished writing you can re-read your answer quickly, checking that you have expressed yourself clearly and accurately. You can also make any last-minute improvements as you read through what you have written.

⇨ Exam practice 4

① This is an exam-style Question 1 from Paper 2, Section C. Read it through and do your annotation and thinking as if you were going to answer the question in the exam, but do not write anything yet.

In 'November Night, Edinburgh', how does the poet present feelings about winter?'

Poem 1: 'November Night, Edinburgh' by Norman MacCaig

The night tinkles like ice in glasses.
Leaves are glued to the pavement with frost.
The brown air fumes at the shop windows,
Tries the doors, and sidles past.

I gulp down winter raw. The heady
Darkness swirls with tenements.
In a brown fuzz of cottonwool
Lamps fade up crags, die into pits.

Frost in my lungs is harsh as leaves
Scraped up on paths. – I look up, there,
A high roof sails, at the mast-head
Fluttering a grey and ragged star.

The world's a bear shrugged in his den.
It's snug and close in the snoring night.
And outside like chrysanthemums
The fog unfolds its bitter scent.

---

② Read this extract from a student response to Question 1.

What first strikes me about the poem is how it evokes the cold. The speaker refers to the ice, frost and how winter tastes 'raw'. This is a vivid description of how cold air feels in your throat on a bitter winter's night. He goes on to say that the frost feels like dead winter leaves, dry and cold, but this image is also very visual as it makes me 'see' the autumn leaves as they lie on city pavements. The whole poem is like a picture of winter but with sensory images and the poet uses the colour brown to indicate the dirty air of the city at night. The words 'cottonwool' and 'snug and close' imply warmth but this contrasts with the reality of the cold icy night. I get the feeling the speaker likes winter and enjoys this contrast. Warmth and life, and spring to come, are symbolised by a hibernating bear 'shrugged in his den'. This is juxtaposed against the cold, bleak winter cityscape. There's a striking image in the last two lines where the poet likens the scent of fog, 'bitter', to that of chrysanthemums. It's striking because in the dead of winter we do not expect to think of a summer flower but it shows that even when winter is at its coldest, the speaker is thinking of summer.

③ How would you improve this response? Consider whether the essay has been successful in the following ways:

- Has the student commented on the poet's use of language, structure and form?
- Has the student supported his points with relevant quotations or details?
- Has the student explained the effect of the poet's methods on the reader?
- What level would you give the extract? Try to explain the reasons behind your decision.

④ Now look at this example Question 2 from Paper 2, Section C. Read it through and do your annotation and thinking as if you were going to answer the question in the exam, but do not write anything yet.

In 'November Night, Edinburgh' and 'Night Photograph', the speakers describe their feelings about a scene at night. What are the similarities and differences between the ways the poets present those feelings?'

Poem 2: 'Night Photograph' by Lavinia Greenlaw
Crossing the Channel at midnight in winter,
coastline develops as distance grows,
then simplifies to shadow, under-exposed.

Points of light – quayside, harbour wall,
the edge of the city –
sink as the surface of the night fills in.

Beyond the boat, the only interruption
is the choppy grey-white we leave behind us,
gone almost before it is gone from sight.

What cannot be pictured is the depth
with which the water moves against itself,
in such abstraction the eye can find

no break, direction or point of focus.
Clearer, and more possible than this,
is the circular horizon.

Sea and sky meet in suspension,
gradual familiar textures of black:
eel-skin, marble, smoke, oil –

---

made separate and apparent by the light
that pours from the sun onto the moon,
the constant white on which these unfixable

layers of darkness thicken and fade.
We are close to land, filtering through
shipping lanes and marker buoys

towards port and its addition of colour.
There is a slight realignment of the planets.
Day breaks at no particular moment.

(5) Read this extract from a student response to Question 2. An examiner has commented on this answer. Read the examiner comments.

In both poems the speakers give realistic, almost photographic, descriptions of the scenes before them. In Poem 1 the scene is a city, Edinburgh, while in Poem 2 the speaker is crossing the English Channel. Both poems take place at night and there is a sense of cold and isolation in both poems, shown in Poem 1 by the poet's use of details – pavements, shop windows – and no people. Similarly in Poem 2 the speaker describes how the quay recedes from sight, leaving only the black-on-black horizon of sea and sky. Both poets contain images of darkness but while in Poem 1 it is a darkness that's 'brown', calling to mind polluted city air, in Poem 2 the darkness is textured and patterned and sensory, offering the speaker a changing skyscape, like an abstract painting. I think the poet in Poem 2 is more visual in her imagery and she creates a sense of mystery, referring to 'what cannot be pictured', whilst in Poem 1 the poet offers a more physical response to night.

Both poems contain images of sailing and in Poem 1 the image 'a high roof sails, at the masthead/Fluttering a grey and ragged star' is incongruous since the speaker describing a city skyline. It makes me think the speaker in Poem 1 has a stronger imagination (chrysanthemums is another incongruous image) than in Poem 2, and is more present throughout the poem, as he refers to 'I' whilst the speaker in the second poem refers to 'we', which makes it more inclusive but also less personal.

Each verse in Poem 1 deals with a different aspect of winter, so the structure underpins the development of the poem, whilst in Poem 2 the poet uses a very free verse structure, with lines broken seemingly at random in the three-line verses, as if free-form. The absence of capital letters at the start of each line in Poem 2 underlines this – the effect is to make us feel like we are witnessing a dream-like reverie, whilst in Poem 1 we feel the speaker's presence more strongly.

Examiner comment

This response would be awarded 7 marks which makes it a Level 4 response. It answers the question fully, comparing several poetic techniques, structure and form. The response provides evidence and there is some exploration of effects. The student also offers insightful and convincing personal interpretations which are based on the effects of language and structure and the comparison is sustained throughout.

(6) Now have a go at answering both questions on pages 135 and 136 yourself. You could attempt to plan and write your answers under timed exam conditions if you wish. Work through the questions as you would in the exam, so re-read the first poem and answer Question 1 then re-read the second poem and answer Question 2.

Acknowledgements

p.4 Lord Byron, from 'When We Two Parted' (1816); **p.8** Percy Bysshe Shelley, from 'Love's Philosophy' (1820); **p.11** Robert Browning, from 'Porphyria's Lover' (1836); **p.15** Elizabeth Barrett Browning, from Sonnet 29 - 'I think of thee' (1850); **p.18** Thomas Hardy, from 'Neutral Tones' (1867); **p.22** Charlotte Mew, from 'The Farmer's Bride' (1916); **p.26** Cecil Day-Lewis, from 'Walking Away' from *Selected Poems*, ed. Jill Balcon (Enitharmon Press, 2004), © C Day Lewis. Reproduced by permission of the publisher; **p.29** Maura Dooley, from 'Letters From Yorkshire' from *Sound Barrier Poems 1982-2002* (Bloodaxe Books, 2002), © Maura Dooley. Reproduced by permission of the publisher; **p.32** Charles Causley, from 'Eden Rock' from *Collected Poems 1951-2000* (Picador, 2000), © Charles Causley. Reproduced by permission of David Higham Ltd; **p.35** Seamus Heaney, from 'Follower' from *Death of a Naturalist* (Faber & Faber, 2006); **p.39** Simon Armitage, from 'Mother, Any Distance' from *Book of Matches* (Faber & Faber, 2001); **p.43** Carol Ann Duffy, from 'Before You Were Mine' from *Mean Time* (Picador, 2013); **p.47** Owen Sheers, from 'Winter Swans' from *Skirrid Hill* (Seren, 2005); **p.50** Daljit Nagra, from 'Singh Song!' from *Look We Have Coming To Dover!* (Faber & Faber, 2007); **p.53** Andrew Waterhouse, from 'Climbing my Grandfather' from *In* (The Rialto, 2000); **p.61** Percy Bysshe Shelley, from 'Ozymandias' (1818); **p.65** William Blake, from 'London' (1794); **p.69** William Wordsworth, from 'The Prelude: stealing the boat' (1850); **p.72** Robert Browning, from 'My Last Duchess' (1842); **p.78** Alfred, Lord Tennyson, from 'The Charge of the Light Brigade' (1854); **p.80** Wilfred Owen, from 'Exposure' (1917); **p.84** Seamus Heaney, from 'Storm on the Island' from *Death of a Naturalist* (Faber & Faber, 2006); **p.86** Ted Hughes, from 'Bayonet Charge' from *GCSE Anthology Moon on the Tides* (Oxford University Press, 2010); **p.91** Simon Armitage, from 'Remains' from *The Not Dead* (Pomona Press, 2008), © Simon Armitage. Reproduced by permission of the publisher; **p.95** Jane Weir, from 'Poppies' from *GCSE Anthology Moon on the Tides* (Oxford University Press, 2010); **p.98** Carol Ann Duffy, from 'War Photographer' from *New Selected Poems 1984-2004* (Picador, 2004); **p.99** Roger Tooth, from 'Graphic content: when photographs of carnage are too upsetting to publish' from *The Guardian* (The Guardian, 23rd July 2014), © Guardian News & Media Ltd 2014, reproduced by permission of the publisher; **p.102** Imtiaz Dharker, from 'Tissue' from *The Terrorist at My Table* (Bloodaxe, 2006), © Imtiaz Dharker. Reproduced by permission of the publisher; **p.105** Carol Rumens, from 'The emigree' from *Poems 1968-2004* (Bloodaxe, 2004); **p.108** Beatrice Garland, from 'Kamikaze' from *The Invention of Fireworks* (Templar Poetry, 2013); **p.111** John Agard, from 'Checking Out Me History' from *Half-Caste and Other Poems* (Hodder Children's Books, 2005); **p.111** Paul Reid, from 'At last, a home for black history' from *The Guardian* (The Guardian, 23rd July 2014), copyright Guardian News & Media Ltd 2014, reproduced by permission of the publisher; **p.121** Marian Collihole,: from 'Impressions of a New Boy' from *Rusty and Friends* (Stainer & Bell, 1980), reproduced by permission of the publisher; **p.125** Carol Ann Duffy, 'In Mrs Tilscher's Class' from *The Other Country* (Picador, 2010); **p.131** Simon Armitage, 'I Am Very Bothered' from *Book of Matches* (Faber & Faber, 2001); **p.135** Norman MacCaig, 'November Night, Edinburgh' from *The Sinai Sort* (The Hogarth Press, 1957); **p.136** Lavinia Greenlaw, 'Night Photograph' from *Night Photograph* (Faber & Faber, 1993).

Photo credits

p.4 © Georgios Kollidas/Fotolia; **p.8** bottom © tdubphoto/Getty Images; **p.9** top, **p.63** top, **p. 66** © nickolae/Fotolia; **p.11** © World History Archive/Alamy; **pp.12/13** © Archivart/Alamy; **p.15** © Classic Image/Alamy; **p.18** © Illustrated London News; **p.20** © Balazs Kovacs Images/Fotolia; **pp.20/21** © Culture-Images/Lebrecht **p.23** © Beryl Peters Collection/Alamy; **p.25** © Allen Donikowski/Getty Images; **p.26** © Keystone Pictures USA/Alamy; **p.28** © by David Hunter/Bloodaxe Books Ltd.; **p.29** © Bloodaxe Books Ltd.; **p.31** © Helen Hotson/Fotolia; **p.34** © jacf5244 – Fotolia; **p.35** © creative/Fotolia; **pp.36/37** © nadezhda1906/Fotolia; **p.38** top © GARY DOAK/Alamy; **pp.38/39** bottom © bara/Fotolia; **p.41** © Bert Hardy/Stringer/Getty Images; **pp.42/43** © Pictorial Press Ltd/Alamy; **p.45** © Ekaterina Myshenko/Fotolia; **p.48** © Derek Adams/Alamy; **p.49** © Nic Cleave Photography/Alamy; **pp.50/51** © avebreakMediaMicro/Fotolia; **p.52** © catgrig/Fotolia; **p.59** © Gilles BASSIGNAC/Gamma-Rapho via Getty Images; **pp.60/61** © Jim Henderson/Alamy; **p.62** © World History Archive/Alamy; **pp.63** bottom © Popova Olga/Fotolia; **p.65** © William Blake/The Bridgeman Art Library/Getty Images; **pp.67, 76/77** © Georgios Kollidas/Fotolia; **p.69** © Stephen Dorey – Bygone Images/Alamy; **p.70** © North Carolina Museum of Art/Corbis; **p.74** © Fine Art Images/HIP/TopFoto; **pp.78/79** © PF-(wararchive)/Alamy; **p.80** © TopFoto; **p.82** © Patryk Kosmider/Fotolia; **pp.84/85** © Richard Cummins/Getty Images; **p.86** top Fox Photos/Getty Images; **pp.86/87** bottom © SOTK2011/Alamy; **p.89** © Purple Pilchards/Alamy; **p.91** © ESSAM AL-SUDANI/AFP/Getty Images; **p.93** © Ozimages/Alamy; **p.95** © Awe Inspiring Images/Fotolia; **p.96** © David Turnley/Corbis; **p.97** © Bettmann/Corbis; **p.100** © Simon Powell/Bloodaxe Books Ltd.; **p.101** © Bloodaxe Books Ltd.; **p.103** © Roman Sigaev/Fotolia; **p.104** © Mark Herreid/Fotolia; **p.105** © victoria p/Fotolia; **p.106** © INTERFOTO/Alamy; **p.108** © The LIFE Images Collection/Getty Images; **p.109** © Michael Putland/Getty Images; **p.111** © gurkoao/Fotolia; **pp.120/121** © Doug Houghton/TopFoto; **p.126** © Tryfonov/Fotolia; **p.131** © andreamuscatello/Fotolia; **p.135** © age fotostock/Alamy; **p.138** © FLPA/Alamy.